TROY HICKS

The Digital Writing Workshop

HEINEMANN
Portsmouth, NH

Heinemann
361 Hanover Street
Portsmouth, NH 03801–3912
www.heinemann.com

Offices and agents throughout the world

© 2009 by Troy Hicks

All rights reserved. No part of this book may be reproduced in any form or by any electronic or mechanical means, including information storage and retrieval systems, without permission in writing from the publisher, except by a reviewer, who may quote brief passages in a review.

"Dedicated to Teachers" is a trademark of Greenwood Publishing Group, Inc.

The author and publisher wish to thank those who have generously given permission to reprint borrowed material:

"Exploring Copyright through Collaborative Wiki Writing" by Troy Hicks originally appeared in *Classroom Notes Plus*, Volume 26, Number 2, October, 2008. Published by the National Council of Teachers of English. Reprinted by permission of the publisher.

Figures 5.7, 5.8 and 5.9 are screenshots from Apple's iTunes® software. Reprinted by permission of Apple Inc.

Figures 5.1, 5.2 and 5.3 are screenshots from Edublogs. Reprinted by permission of Edublogs.

Figure 2.5 is a screenshot from Zotero. Reprinted by permission of Zotero.

Figures 5.4, 5.5 and 5.6 and A.1 and A.2 are screenshots from Wikispaces. Reprinted by permission of Wikispaces.

Adapted from Figure 40.1 "Traits of effective and ineffective writers" from *Writing Reminders: Tools, Tips, and Techniques* by Jim Burke. Copyright © 2003 by Jim Burke. Published by Heinemann. Reprinted by permission.

Library of Congress Cataloging-in-Publication Data
Hicks, Troy.
    The digital writing workshop / Troy Hicks.
        p. cm.
    Includes bibliographical references and index.
    ISBN-13: 978-0-325-02674-9
    ISBN-10: 0-325-02674-2
    1. English language—Composition and exercises—Study and teaching (Secondary)—United States.   2. English language—Rhetoric Study and teaching (Secondary).
3. English language—Computer-assisted instruction.   4. Educational technology.
I. Title.
    LB1631.H494 2009
    808′.0420785—dc22

                                                                    2009018395

Editor: James Strickland
Production editor: Sonja S. Chapman
Typesetter: Publishers' Design and Production Services, Inc.
Cover design: Night & Day Design
Author photo: Sara Beauchamp-Hicks
Manufacturing: Valerie Cooper

Printed in the United States of America on acid-free paper
13 12 11 10 09 PAH 1 2 3 4 5

TO HEATHER,
FOR EVERYTHING.
LOVE, TROY

Contents

Foreword

Several years ago a six-year-old named Danny asked if I wanted to "watch his book." I was puzzled, but let him put his sticky hand in mine and lead me to the computer along a wall in his first-grade classroom where his digital story played to a group of classmates. As Danny's voice said, "Here comes the train!" the students joined in, just like in a read-aloud, chanting with the story then hitting play to hear it again. With a scanner and a handheld microphone his teacher had shown him how to rework his writing into a movie. As you suspect, engagement for writing soared in that classroom. Writers couldn't wait to create.

Since then I've led my high school seniors through digital stories and commentaries, through text study on YouTube to sharing drafts in a class blog, but there are plenty of tools I've kept at a distance. Wikis, shared spaces and documents, feeds and readers: it all sounds a bit like a Dr. Seuss picture book where folks I don't recognize speak a language unfamiliar and a bit scary. I can't get the help I need from our overtaxed technology department, so I've avoided even free tools to rely on what's familiar.

And then along comes Troy Hicks' *The Digital Writing Workshop*.

In clean, clear prose that unravels the labyrinth of new terms and applications, Troy guides us toward a writing workshop for this age. His steady, smart advice eases the transition from the elements of writing workshop we know matter to the tools that can take each to a new place, one comfortably familiar, but with a decidedly updated feel. And this man has his priorities straight. He says, "I argue here and throughout this book that if we engage students in real writing tasks and we use technology in such a way that it complements their innate need to find purposes and audiences for their work, we can have them engaged in a digital writing process that focuses first on the writer, then on the writing, and lastly on the technology" (8).

If this were merely a how-to guide for programs it would have a shelf life like milk, quickly passed by as emerging technologies take root, then splinter into new ideas. But this book has vision. Troy reminds us of the solid thinking behind workshop teaching that will lead us long past the particular tools described so thoroughly here. I read with my computer beside me checking the sites Troy listed, creating a wiki for my class, then my own RSS feed, and bouncing a little in my chair as I played with tools I'd been too cowardly to access. I know I'm laps behind Troy Hicks, but I see him cheering me on, hear his voice on these pages saying, "Join me! I'll show you how." Instead of waiting for district professional development that will never come, I have Troy's thinking to guide me.

Troy considers the pillars of workshop teaching (student choice, active revision, author's craft, publication, and broader visions of assessment) through a digital lens. When considering ideas to explore in writing, Troy shows how using an RSS feed individualized for each writer allows students to access relevant current thinking related to their interests. This has potential far beyond lists in a writer's notebook. And he goes farther, imagining the RSS feed for SSR. I chuckled thinking how we've barely made the leap to allowing magazines alongside books in our rooms and Troy imagines an eclectic, student-determined gathering of what to read and how much of it. I love it when colleagues press my thinking. Troy shows how using a classroom wiki engages writers in conversations that are far broader than "turn and talk," and are captured as text so they can be reread and considered as the draft emerges, perhaps as part of a blogfolio. The chapters on publication and assessment show that each line of thinking was crafted with students in classrooms like yours and mine. He anticipates problems and shows solutions. I wish he taught in the classroom next door, but his book allows me to be beside him.

The larger point of the book—that our writers can achieve more, understand more, and discover more using digital tools, than in our traditional writing workshop—was inspiring. Troy describes digital newscasts, book trailers, and public service announcements as "textured composition, one in which many subtle aspects of the work that could simply be considered as background noise actually magnify work in ways that just an author reading her piece could not achieve on her own" (73). I want my students to live in that writing world.

In Troy's book we have not just words, but a companion website. Not just the latest tools and projects that show what students can do with them, but the layers of thinking beneath the surface of flash, the foundation of principles in a solid writing workshop. Troy delivers the fine details and the big vision. He understands the theory we know in our hearts.

Thank you, Troy, for new tools, for new possibilities.

—Penny Kittle

Acknowledgments

When beginning graduate school a few years ago, I was unable to even conceive of the idea of writing a book, despite my long-held desire to write one. There are two significant reasons that I have been able to write this page of acknowledgments and share with you the book that follows.

First, I thank my wife, Heather. As all of my friends and colleagues know, she was diagnosed with an aggressive form of breast cancer in January 2006 yet never looked back. She continued to live her life and love her family until her body failed her in May 2008. Throughout that journey, she continued to support me as I worked and completed my research and writing. Without her, my dissertation would have never been finished, and I don't know that I would have gained the confidence to write this book.

Second, I thank the many colleagues and friends that I have gained as a result of attending graduate school and, as a part of that experience, working at the Michigan State University Writing Center and joining the Red Cedar Writing Project. My mentor, Janet Swenson, offered me opportunities through this work that led me to explore digital writing in a variety of ways. Through those connections, I was able to join the larger network of the National Writing Project, and nearly everything discussed in this book comes in some way from how these colleagues have taught me to think about how to teach digital writing. In particular, I thank the following:

- all of my colleagues with whom I have worked over the past six years, and especially those who have contributed materials to this book or have invited me to link to their work: Paul Allison, Sara Beauchamp, Aram Kabodian, Clifford Lee, Heather Lewis, Sharon Murchie, Melissa Pomerantz, Shannon Powell, Dawn Reed, and Chris Sloan

- my writing group buddies who have been with me from the start of my dissertation through the final proofreading of this book: Jim Fredricksen and Rob Petrone
- the teachers involved in Red Cedar Writing Project's 2008–9 Title II professional development grant, Project WRITE, and especially the project facilitator, Liz Webb, who always encouraged me to make the connections between literacy and technology explicit to all the "nontechies" in the group

From Heinemann, I thank Jim Strickland, Sonja Chapman, Elizabeth Tripp, Lisa Luedeke, Jill Harden, and Stephanie Turner, all of whom helped me prepare or revise this manuscript in some way. Also, I thank Jim Burke both for the many professional texts that he has written about the teaching of writing as well as for his permission to adapt his list of traits of effective and ineffective writers for this book.

Most importantly, I recognize my children—Tyler, Lexi, and Cooper—and I thank my immediate family, in-laws, and best friends, all of whom have supported me in my personal and professional life through an incredibly difficult time: Ron and Carol Hicks; Barry and Becki Hicks; Gary and Diana Catlin; Matt and Kristen LeBaron; and Steve and Alana Tuckey.

And, as nearly all writers note in their acknowledgments, there are many more thanks to be made but not enough space to make them. So, please know that if you have been a part of my life in the past six years, and have been one of the many who have asked me, "How is the book going?" then I offer my thanks to you, too.

Imagining a Digital Writing Workshop

Like you, I am a teacher of writing. We rely on decades of experience from practitioners and researchers who have formulated, implemented, written about, changed, and tried again their ideas about teaching writing in a workshop format. And all of us continue to learn every day what it means to be a teacher of writing as we listen to our students, shape our responses and lessons around their needs, and assess the work that they have completed.

Teacher researchers such as Donald Graves, Donald Murray, Lucy Calkins, Nancie Atwell, Katie Wood Ray, Jim Burke, Ralph Fletcher, and Penny Kittle—among the countless numbers of us who have employed their ideas in our own classrooms—have developed the writing workshop into a theoretically sound and pedagogically useful model for teaching writing. While we each can and should make our own list of particular ideas about what constitutes the philosophy of the writing workshop in our own classroom, I feel that we can generally agree that it relies on a core set of principles that center on students as writers, where we "teach the writer, not the writing" (Calkins 1994), as many of the aforementioned authors would remind us. There are a number of core principles that proponents of the writing workshop approach advocate, and I offer my summary of them here:

- student choice about topic and genre
- active revision (constant feedback between peer and teacher)
- author's craft as a basis for instruction (through minilessons and conferences)

- publication beyond classroom walls
- broad visions of assessment that include both process and product

These principles of the workshop approach provide thousands of teachers, like you and me, the building blocks for engaging our writers, day in and day out. These elements are all present, in some fashion, in work presented by the other authors noted earlier, in workshops and presentations that teachers share, and in the core beliefs of our professional organizations, such as the National Council of Teachers of English and the National Writing Project.

Moreover, these principles allow us to explore the wide variety of learning-to-write, writing-to-learn, and genre studies under the umbrella of the writing workshop. For instance, teacher researchers have begun to explore multigenre work (Putz 2006; Romano 2000) and writing on demand as components of the writing workshop (Gere, Christenbury, and Sassi 2005). These trends are promising, as they represent our work as a field moving beyond typical critiques of the writing workshop such as that it focused only on expressive writing or that it didn't force students to fully consider the context, purpose, and audience for their work across different writing situations.

And, in the past five years or so, more professional articles and books than I can cite here have begun exploring another key idea in composition studies: newer literacies and technologies. This is promising, and it's good to know that teachers are utilizing computers and the Internet in ways that they had not before. Sara Kajder asks, however, "Is that enough? Does doing something old with new technology mean that I'm teaching with technology and that I'm doing so in a way as to really improve the reading and writing skills of the students in my classroom?" (2007, 214). Her answer, as well as mine, would be no. When we simply bring a traditional mind-set to literacy practices, and not a mind-set that understands new literacies (an idea developed by Colin Lankshear and Michele Knobel, which I elaborate on later) into the process of digital writing, we cannot make the substantive changes to our teaching that need to happen in order to embrace the full potential of collaboration and design that digital writing offers.

What do I mean by changing our mind-set? The image in Figure 1.1 is from the classroom of my colleague Aram Kabodian, a middle school language arts teacher in East Lansing, Michigan, and technology liaison for the Red Cedar Writing Project at Michigan State University. It invites us to consider a question: what happens in the writing workshop when we introduce digital writing tools and processes? By bringing a laptop into this writing workshop, it creates new

Middle school students engaged in digital movie making

FIGURE 1.1

opportunities and challenges in the teaching of writing that the previous authors discussing the writing workshop model or the uses of particular technology tools have not fully addressed. Study this photo for a moment, and consider what happens in a typical writing workshop, where students work on their own pieces, offer peer response, and bring their writing to publication. Then consider the following questions about this particular moment in Kabodian's digital writing workshop. As you study the photo, you should know that Kabodian was inviting students to create public service announcements (PSAs) with a moviemaking program, and examples of his students' work can be found at akabodian7.pbworks.com/PSA.

Here are some questions to consider based on this snapshot of a digital writing workshop:

- What writing processes and expectations are the same as they have always been for print texts? What has changed?
- Who is (or who are) the writer(s) of this text? The girls who are seated, or the girl leaning in and using the trackpad? Who gets credit for having *composed*—a term that Yancey (2008) uses to broaden our notions of what it means to write with text, images, sounds, and video—this text? How is that credit assessed—as a part of the process, as a part of the final product, or both?
- What do the writers need to know about the topics related to their PSAs? Where do they find information that is credible and timely? How do they determine whether this information is, in fact, credible and timely?
- What rhetorical skills related to informative and persuasive writing does a student need to have in order to compose a PSA? What technical skills does she need to have to be able to find or create images for a digital movie? What writing skills does she need to have to compose and then record the narration for the PSA?
- How do writers track and manage the images and information that they find as they are researching so as to cite them properly and make sure they are employing them within the boundaries of fair use for copyrighted material?
- What behaviors need to be taught during the writing workshop, and what dispositions do writers need to have in order to work collaboratively as well as offer constructive responses to digital writing?
- How does assessment work when writers are no longer singularly responsible for their text, both in terms of finding preexisting materials that others have created and they repurpose as well as in terms of who actually does particular kinds of work on the text? For instance, if one person gathers images, another writes the script for the narration, and a third compiles the timeline for the PSA, have they all engaged equally and fully in the writing process?
- How do students distribute their work in a particular multimedia format, gain access to the Internet and sites for publishing such as a blog or wiki, and follow the acceptable use policy of their school? Moreover, as Will Richardson suggests, how does students' work get shared online so it can be "added to the conversation and potentially used to teach others?" (2006, 132).

These questions have consequences for how we teach, the tasks we ask students to engage in, and the tools that we ask them to use. And our answers to these questions help us frame our own pedagogy as an approach to teaching in the digital writing workshop.

The Purpose of This Book

In the past decade or so—and especially in the past three or four years—we've all noticed a change both in the computer technology that we use each day, including our cell phones and other handheld devices, as well as in how we are using those devices to communicate with one another. Newer technologies and media-rich environments are enabling what have been called *newer*, *multiple*, or *digital* literacies. We, as teachers of writing, are still coming to understand how these literacies interact with—and sometimes change—the principles of the writing workshop. A number of texts have explored the ways in which particular digital writing tools work, and ways to engage students in digital writing, yet I do not feel as if they offer a vision for what it means to teach in a digital writing workshop.

This book aims to fill that void.

By integrating the core principles of the writing workshop with those surrounding emerging technologies for writing, this book connects the writing workshop approach with the integration of newer technologies such as blogs, wikis, social networks, podcasts, and digital stories. By discussing these technologies through the framework of the five principles of the writing workshop noted previously—allowing for student choice, encouraging active revision, studying author's craft, publishing beyond the classroom, and broadening our understandings of assessment—I intend to place digital writing tools in a context that those of us familiar with the writing workshop approach can understand and apply them to create better writers.

In order to do this, I first provide some background in this introductory chapter about the specifics of the writing workshop approach and what others have called digital writing. I do this both to establish where I am coming from and also to think carefully about what, at the core, these two branches of writing studies have to say to one another. Then, I briefly discuss implications for reimagining the writing workshop, given how digital literacies complicate the relationship between text, reader, and writer. Finally, I outline the remainder of the book so that you can see where next to direct your attention for your own personal learning.

The Writing Workshop Approach

Many teacher researchers define and describe the writing workshop in a variety of ways. Lucy Calkins reminds us that the writing workshop requires us "to anticipate how we will initiate, scaffold, and guide the classroom community toward an ever-deepening involvement . . . [by selecting] rituals, arrangements, and classroom structures" (1994, 183). And "when writers write every day, they begin to compose even when they are not composing. They enter a 'constant state of composition'" (Graves 1994, 104). The writing workshop, at its core, centers on students as writers and provides them the time and space to engage in writing.

Over the past thirty years and especially since the publication of Calkins' *The Art of Teaching Writing* (1986 and 1994) and Nancie Atwell's *In the Middle* (1987 and 1998), teachers have continued to teach with the workshop approach. Along with the exemplary work of the National Writing Project, numerous local, state, and national professional organizations find their publications and conferences peppered with references to such ideas as *conferring*, *minilessons*, *running records*, and *portfolios*—words introduced to a generation of students who are now becoming writing teachers themselves. And, while I would like to believe that the writing workshop has come of age, and is present in classrooms throughout the country, I know from personal experience, conversations with colleagues, and the amount of our professional literature that still devotes itself to discussing writing workshop approaches that this is not the case.

Why is it, then, that the writing workshop approach and language are not a part of every writing teacher's repertoire? Part of it may be that we are engaging students in writing, but not through a workshop approach. For instance, Katie Wood Ray and Lester Laminack argue:

> I have seen many classrooms where students "do the writing process,"
> and the focus is on *pieces of writing* and how to take those pieces of
> writing through each step of the process—prewriting, drafting, revision,
> editing, and publication. . . . This down-the-line kind of emphasis can be

contrasted to a writing workshop where the focus is very much on *writers* rather than on the process that leads to finished pieces. Now, without a doubt, students in writing workshops utilize all the steps of the writing process—their teachers gives them lots of instruction around the process so they can get pieces ready for publications—but it's not as though they really *do* the writing process. It's more like they *use* the writing process to get other things done. (2001, 4)

There can be a world of difference between doing and using the writing process when it comes to our philosophy about teaching writing. That is, if we focus on making individual pieces of writing better, then we fail to see the larger goal of our instruction—helping students become better writers. Hence the mantra "Teach the writer, not the writing" (although, through many discussions with my Red Cedar Writing Project colleague Liz Webb about professional development and how we frame this idea to our fellow teachers, we have come to say, "Teach the writer, then the writing").

As I mentioned earlier, there may not be a general consensus around every single element of what is or is not a part of the writing workshop approach. That, however, is not as important as the fact that the approach itself has been proven to work in countless classrooms and, whether we agree it is a valid measure or not, in the test scores of the children who participate in such classrooms. For instance, recent work through the National Writing Project's (2006) Local Sites Research Initiative showed that students of teachers who had attended an NWP summer institute outperformed their peers in classes of teachers who had not attended a summer institute in all six traits of writing measured, save one, in which there was no difference. Also, in a meta-analysis of studies, a number of writing strategies are verified to improve student writing, many of which are used in a writing workshop approach, including "planning, revising, and editing," collaboration, goal setting, prewriting, inquiry activities, and the study of models (Graham and Perin 2006).

We all know that formulas—be they five paragraphs, six traits, or any number of stages in the process—still exist. Moreover, they permeate our curriculum guides, bookshelves, and professional discussions. They are not going away. Yet writing is a complicated, recursive, and ever-changing process. With the addition of technology, that process changes even more.

Like Ray and Laminack, I often talk with teachers who feel that they are doing the writing process, yet their students seem uninterested in writing. I do not propose that technology is or ever will be the silver bullet for solving apathy, although I know that many people (especially those who market computer-based essay scoring or automated reading tests) make that claim. Instead, I argue here and throughout this book that if we engage students in real writing tasks and we use technology in such a way that it complements their innate need to find purposes and audiences for their work, we can have them engaged in a digital writing process that focuses first on the writer, then on the writing, and lastly on the technology. As we shift our attention from the technology back to the writer, we begin to take the stance of not just integrating computers or using a particular program and begin to think about how to structure our digital writing workshop.

Newer, Multiple, and Digital Literacies: The Theories Behind Digital Writing

As writing has changed with computer-mediated, networked environments, so too have our conceptions about what it means to be literate. Although I could spend significant time discussing broader theories of literacy learning, and the implications that each has for how we pursue the teaching of writing, suffice it to say here that I subscribe to a sociocultural perspective that began gaining traction about the same time that the writing workshop approach to teaching did. This perspective on literacy learning holds that individuals learn how to read and write for specific purposes, in specific contexts, and that there is a commonly accepted form of discourse that schools adhere to in their teaching of reading and writing. From this perspective, then, it is important to teach students both how to read and write as well as how to be critical of what they are reading and writing. In other words, writing—whether in school or out, whether on a computer or a pad of paper—is an individual act mediated by the world around us, an act that we must be constantly conscious of while we engage in it.

Thus, there are many different angles to literacy learning that can inform our thinking about what it means to write with technology and how writing is changed by technology. Three of them pertinent to understanding digital writing include Lankshear and Knobel's "new literacies," the New London Group's "pedagogy of multiliteracies," and Gilster's "digital literacies." Looking at each one of these in some detail will provide a broad look at what it can mean to be literate in the twenty-first century.

The first theory, new literacies, developed by Michele Knobel and Colin Lankshear (2006), outlines how newer technologies and social norms are changing what it means to be literate, suggesting that there are two mind-sets that accompany old and new ways of envisioning literacy:

> We distinguish between two broad mindsets that people use to understand and orient themselves toward the world. One mindset approaches the contemporary world as being much the same now as it has been in the past, only a bit more "technologized"—it has digital technologies added to it, but is nonetheless to be understood and related to more or less as we have done for the past 200 to 300 years.... The other mindset sees the world as having changed very significantly from how it was, necessitating a different approach from the one used in the past.... It recognizes cyberspace as a fact of the new world, to be taken into account along with the physical world, but believes that cyberspace operates on the basis of different assumptions and values from physical space. (80)

The differences in these mind-sets, especially for us as writing teachers, make us question our fundamental beliefs about learning. For instance, it is a difference between trusting only books from the library and being open to having students cite from (and, perhaps, write in) Wikipedia, between posting our assignments and students' work on a closed course management system and using a blog that parents and students can see from home or school. These are significant changes for us to consider, and Knobel and Lankshear remind us that we may need "a different approach from the one used in the past," one that inevitably involves networks, collaboration, and shared visions of how knowledge is made and distributed differently in digital spaces.

The second theory, a pedagogy of multiliteracies, emerged from the work of the New London Group (2000), and it suggests that learners become literate by engaging in four stages of literacy learning that examine "designs of meaning." In other words, how do particular communities of people produce and consume texts? For writing teachers, the concept of being multiliterate means that we need to both teach linguistically diverse students and honor the languages and dialects that they bring while also introducing them to the larger discourse of schooling and the community. Also, it means teaching about visual, aural, spatial, gestural, and other literacies that move beyond basic print texts. Together, this need to recognize linguistic diversity and engage in multimodal production of texts complicates the teaching of writing (or, to use a term that a number of scholars including Yancey [2008] use instead to describe the act of writing now, *composing*). Writing is, quite simply, about more than putting words on paper (or screen), but about the many ways in which language, culture, and technology interact.

Then there are documents that outline what have been called "electronic," "twenty-first-century," or, the term I prefer, "digital" literacies. A search on the phrase **digital literacy**, coined by Paul Gilster, now generates a list of dozens of books from Amazon and 392,000 hits from Google. As outlined in his "Primer on Digital Literacy," Gilster (1997) suggests that evaluating content, mastering search engines, and setting up personal news feeds are the building blocks for being digitally literate. These types of skills are reflected in numerous recent curriculum documents and policy statements, yet they refer only to the consumption of information, not its production. In order to better understand the creation of digital texts, the Writing in Digital Environments (WIDE) Research Center Collective (2005) suggests that we think of writing as networked. The researchers in the Collective argue that "[c]onnectivity allows writers to access and participate more seamlessly and instantaneously within web spaces and to distribute writing to large and widely dispersed audiences." In conjunction with Gilster's definition of digital literacy, where students carefully gather and consume digital texts, the WIDE Research Center Collective's ideas suggest that it is just as important for writers to share their own digital texts as it is for them to consume the texts produced by others.

New literacies. Multiliteracies. Digital literacies. Digital writing. It all continues to evolve rapidly, and as writing teachers we need to hold on to some solid ground, some practices that we know work when it comes to teaching writing. This is where the writing workshop model for teaching becomes a key component in how we can help our students learn to be smart digital writers. And, by defining *digital writing*, I borrow from the forthcoming text *Because Digital Writing Matters* (DeVoss, Hicks, and the National Writing Project): digital writing consists of "compositions created with, and oftentimes for, a computer or other device that is connected to the Internet." This is a broad definition and includes everything from instant messages to word-processed documents attached to an email, from slide show presentations to video and audio productions. While it is difficult to pin down exactly what digital writing *is*, in some ways worrying about categorizing digital writing does not matter as much anymore, because nearly all writing that we do is digital in some way; whether we get information from the Internet that informs how we develop the plot of a story, or see a commercial that helps us think of a creative idea to reach our audience in a presentation, nearly all writing today is informed by, if not created with, digital writing tools including websites, software packages, a variety of media sources, and networked communication. Thus, when we ask students to be writers in this age, we are inherently asking them to be digital writers. Therefore, our pedagogy needs to acknowledge this shift and adopt a perspective that honors and integrates digital writing into our classrooms.

Framing Your Digital Writing Workshop

There are many reports and sets of professional and curricular standards that outline the need to connect literacy and technology, yet perhaps none does this so succinctly as the "Neglected 'R'" report (National Commission on Writing in America's Schools and Colleges 2003), which argues that we need to develop a national technology and writing policy, one that includes hardware and software as well as professional development for teachers. Since both the technologies for writing as well as the nature of writing itself continue to change, we need a framework for understanding how to teach writing that is consistent with our current model of teaching in the writing workshop and also integrates newer literacies and technologies.

In order to do this, we must build upon our existing knowledge about the writing workshop, as it can help us reach this goal of using technology in pedagogically sound and sustainable ways. By taking the model of the writing workshop and repurposing it for a new approach to teaching digital writing, we have an opportunity to meet these ambitious goals.

Therefore, I have chosen to focus on the five principles of the writing workshop that have direct implications for teaching digital writing. These are the pillars of the writing workshop that will not change. However, the way that we approach them as we write in digital environments will change. These five principles capture most of what we, as writing teachers, feel are the important components of our workshops, and thus I've organized the rest of the book around them.

Overview of the Book

Because I chose to build the framework for this book around the five core principles of the writing workshop and then layer in discussions of the tools used to support them, the next five chapters of the book each highlight one of the principles and reframe it in light of newer literacies and technologies for digital writing. Each chapter examines tools that can be used to support these principles in action and concludes with a section called "Looking Ahead" that offers additional ideas for how to extend the tools or use other web-based technologies for what Richardson (2006) calls the "read/write web," where readers can easily contribute comments on existing materials or create and share their own texts, images, audio, and video.

- Chapter 2, "Fostering Choice and Inquiry Through RSS, Social Book-marking, and Blogging," demonstrates how new options for gathering, tagging, and saving information allow students to make their own choices as they pursue and write about topics of personal interest.
- Chapter 3, "Conferring Through Blogs, Wikis, and Collaborative Word Processors," examines the process of conferring and how it changes for students and teachers through web-based tools such as blogs, wikis, and collaborative word processors.
- Chapter 4, "Examining Author's Craft Through Multimedia Composition," combines a discussion on author's craft through what we already know about elements such as leads, snapshots, transitions, repetition, and idea development with multimedia compositions such as podcasts and digital stories.
- Chapter 5, "Designing and Publishing Digital Writing," discusses new modes of publication and distribution for digital texts, including audio and video formats that still rely heavily on the recursive processes of brainstorming, drafting, revising, and editing.
- Chapter 6, "Enabling Assessment over Time with Digital Writing Tools," returns to the constant question of assessment and how digital writing can rely on traditional elements of formative and summative assessment, yet also requires us to rethink how we assess writing.
- The closing chapter, "Creating Your Digital Writing Workshop," revisits the major themes developed in each of the previous chapters, asking broadly, "What does it mean to be a teacher of writing in the twenty-first century?" while delivering a framework for thinking about that question, too.
- Finally, the appendix, "Exploring Copyright Through Collaborative Wiki Writing," which originally appeared in slightly different form in NCTE's *Classroom Notes Plus* (Hicks 2008), offers a practical set of lessons for how to integrate a digital writing tool, the wiki, with a key concept in understanding digital writing: copyright.

And, on that topic of copyright, which is reiterated throughout this text, there are many good resources on fair use in education that I recommend you review to be sure you are using the work of others appropriately, most recently the *Code of Best Practices in Fair Use for Media Literacy Education*, available at mediaeducationlab.com/sites/mediaeducationlab.com/files/CodeofBest PracticesinFairUse.pdf (Center for Social Media 2008). In fact, the entire Media Education Lab website (mediaeducationlab.com/) has a number of resources that are worth exploring as you invite your students to create digital writing and consider fair-use provisions in that process.

The appendix of this book is a perfect example of how my understanding of this topic—as well as many other ideas related to digital writing—continues to evolve. For instance, when I wrote the article that is in the appendix, I wrote about the fact that teachers should be extremely careful about the use of copyrighted works. That is the message I had been hearing for years. Then, in the course of finishing this book, two events helped me rethink my understandings of copyright. In a webcast of *Teachers Teaching Teachers* on January 14, 2009, hosts Paul Allison and Susan Ettenheim discussed aspects of fair use with one of the authors of the fair use guide, Peter Jaszi (archived episodes are available at teachersteachingteachers.org/). From that discussion, I gained insights into ways that students and teachers are, under the provisions of fair use, actually able to use copyrighted works in a variety of contexts. Then, a few weeks later, I attended EduCon 2.1 at the Science Leadership Academy in Philadelphia and heard a teacher, Kristin Hokanson, along with one of the other authors of the guide, Renee Hobbs, discuss fair use and show numerous examples that, a year earlier, I would have thought to be a copyright violation. In short, my thinking changed nearly overnight, and I look back at the original draft of my appendix, written many months before I completed this book, and see the many ways I would now add fair use as a part of the lesson. I hope you can implement these ideas when you teach your students about copyright.

All of this is just to say that digital writing—both in content and in form—is malleable. Just when you think you understand everything about copyright, for instance, you begin to see it in a new way. Or, once you think you have mastered how to post something on a wiki, the interface changes and adds new features. Perhaps this is what I like most about being engaged in the teaching of digital writing: every day brings something new. And, thus, the lessons and ideas presented in this book are done so in a manner that, I hope, invites you to see them as exemplars of how to engage in the teaching of digital writing and not as processes to be followed in lockstep, because things continue to change.

Throughout the text, then, you will find examples from students and teachers with whom I have collaborated over the past few years, mostly through the National Writing Project. These lesson plans and links both provide you examples of teaching and learning writing in a digital age and serve as proof that we are all still learning. As I often joke with teachers in my preservice classes or professional development workshops, I am only one step ahead of those with whom I work. Many times, they will ask a question about a particular element of technology or an aspect of digital writing that I have not considered. I seek an answer, share it with them, and then we all figure out the next set of questions to ask. And, as the list of questions about Kabodian's picture in Figure 1.1 demonstrates, the questions about the technical aspects of how to do a particular task with a digital writing tool are usually eclipsed by the questions about how to teach and assess the digital writing itself. The important point is to keep posing questions.

So, please approach this book as a conversation with a colleague, a conversation that we can engage in both in these pages, as writer and reader, and online, where you can take the role of writer, and I the reader, communicating through digital writing. As you read, and engage in digital writing with your students, please share your questions, comments, and ideas. As a part of that continuing conversation, I also invite you to join me on this book's social network at digitalwritingworkshop.ning.com/.

Let's begin the journey.

Fostering Choice and Inquiry Through RSS, Social Bookmarking, and Blogging

Extending the thinking of Lucy Calkins, Nancie Atwell, and others who have suggested that students keep writer's notebooks, in which they can compose questions and explore their passions, the idea of inquiry and choice—a defining element of the writing workshop approach—allows students to pick topics, explore genres and styles, develop pieces, and select publication opportunities. It permeates the very essence of the workshop. Students may choose to build upon an idea presented in a minilesson, but do not have to. They can accept the advice given to them by a peer or a teacher, yet they remain in control of their writing. Choice, within reason, forms the foundation of a writing workshop; a firm belief that students can and will, with guidance, make appropriate choices as writers directs our thinking as teachers.

Within this context of choice, we have become keenly aware of a number of pressures that our students face, too. We can no longer allow them to write just stories and poems; we must teach them the forms of nonfiction writing as well, specifically that of writing on demand. State content-level standards often name a number of genres that students should read and write in, sometimes even specifying technologies such as blogs, wikis, or digital stories. These new demands, while sometimes burdensome, can be generative for us as teachers since they require that we think about multiple genres, audiences, and purposes with our students. More importantly for the purposes of this text, these demands require us to think about the ways in which we can engage students in digital writing and about how sharing writing online can become a key component of our workshop approach.

What, then, are some of the shifts that have happened in our understanding of the composing process that make a focus on digital writing in the writing workshop that much more compelling?

First, we need to examine the "raw materials" (Warlick 2005) from which digital writers gain insight, develop ideas, choose details, and understand genre. It used to be that our students had very few sources for finding these raw materials, most of which were confined to the school or local library. Today, information continues to grow not only from day to day, but minute by minute. From traditional news to citizen journalism, from academic titles to self-published books, and from major media outlets to whoever can post a video on YouTube, we are inundated with more and more information. We ask students to begin by writing from their lives. Today, students' lives consist of a variety of information sources, and teachers need to understand how to teach students to best access, organize, and utilize that information.

Second, our understanding of what constitutes literacy continues to change. As noted in Chapter 1, we as teachers continue to develop more sophisticated notions of what literacy is and how students enact it in their daily lives. The term *new literacies* encompasses both the technical stuff of new literacies—knowing particular gadgets, web services, and other technology-based tools—as well as the ethos stuff, or the general mind-set toward a more open and collaborative process of literacy learning (Knobel and Lankshear 2006; Lankshear and Knobel 2006), which must be in place for us to consider a literacy new. For instance, teachers could invite students to use a blog to post comments on a teacher-initiated discussion. Yet this would not be new, as it is simply using a traditional pedagogy (teacher-led discussion) with a new technology. Instead, if students used blogging in the ways that bloggers do—to reflect on their own ideas, comment on other blogs, and synthesize their readings from other sources—this would make the process new in the sense that students would be utilizing the full capacity of blogs as a literacy practice, not just replicating traditional practices in an online space.

What does this mean in everyday practice for us as writing teachers? Let's think about a specific example: the research paper. Like many writers, I first learned how to do research in elementary school, and the process involved a topic that my teacher selected for me, books that my librarian selected, and a series of note cards and outline pages that were fairly well scripted. This process took a total of two to three weeks, in which time we moved from book to note card, from note card to outline, from outline to handwritten draft, and (at least by the time I got to middle school) from handwritten draft to a final draft, produced over a few days of typing on the word processor.

Today, what does it mean for students to do research? Left to their own devices, it could begin and end with a Google search, yet that is not enough for students who should be developing information literacy. There are options that teachers can use to help guide students through this process. One such idea is by designing a WebQuest-style activity, described in detail at webquest.org/index .php. While I appreciate the WebQuest model, and I recognize that many teachers rely on it for structuring Internet-based research, it seems to rely too heavily on teacher-made plans for basic information gathering instead of explicitly guiding students through the process of discovery and collaboration with digital writing tools. We can do better given the tools we now have available with the read/write web.

In an activity about censorship, Sara Beauchamp, a teacher at Negaunee High School and technology liaison for the Upper Peninsula Writing Project, has designed a wiki page that has a number of tasks that ask students to visit other websites, view multimedia, discuss what they have found, and then contribute to the group's understanding about the topic: nhsenglish9.wikispaces.com/ Censorship+Activity. She invites students to literally copy and paste the text from the wiki page into a Google document that they then share within their small group and can contribute to over the course of the unit of study. Each student adds different parts and revises sections that his peers have contributed. By framing the research process for her students, and then inviting them to engage with one another through digital writing tools, Beauchamp guides them through the research process, helps them keep track of their sources, and encourages them to collaboratively develop new understandings about censorship. Instead of having students do a lone WebQuest, or even a group WebQuest in which different people contribute different elements of information to the overall report, Beauchamp works with her students to help them grow as digital writers who produce their own texts and who are not just consumers of information.

While some elements of our curriculum require us to engage all students in similar topics, like the Beauchamp activity, research and writing can also be self-directed based on students' own inquiry and choice in topics. From an initial Google search, a few pages could be reviewed and some chunks of text copied and pasted into a word processor and cited. A trip to the library could involve searches through an electronic catalog, zeroing in on one or two books that were especially useful, with the possibility that the books could be viewed on the screen. Writing could take place on a computer, sometimes fully online through a web-based word processor, where collaborators could revise and edit one another's work. Drafts could be posted to a blog or wiki, while final drafts could be submitted as email attachments.

While this second scenario may not be common for all writers, it is common for some and it is beginning to become more the norm for many. Composing an entire paper in a completely online environment is not out of the question if a writer has regular access to the Internet. Both scenarios, however, from our time collecting note cards to our students' time gathering electronic pieces of text, require a set of critical sensibilities about gathering, organizing, and integrating information into our writing, especially our nonfiction writing. Yet there are many elements in each process that can, without careful consideration, become meaningless tasks and not contribute to our students' writing development.

With this in mind, I now turn to three specific tools that you and your students can use to organize and reflect on the mass quantities of information that we are faced with each day. While I do not list how-to steps for these particular technologies (see this book's social network site, digitalwritingworkshop.ning.com/, for links to online tutorials), I do provide a general sense of what each of these read/write web tools can do for writers in a workshop environment. By remembering the foundational component of choice, and by helping students make wise choices about how to gather and organize information, we can integrate really simple syndication (RSS), social bookmarking, and blogs into our approach to teaching in the digital writing workshop.

As the amount of information continues to grow, we need to teach student writers better ways to handle what they choose to receive. Through the read/write web tools of social bookmarking and RSS, students can decide what information they want to come to them and how best to manage it. Of course, this forces us to consider how students can, and probably will, shut out alternative sources of information, ones that may further support or push against the students' worldviews. Keeping a balance between the types of sources—from academic journals to the news media to individual bloggers—will allow students to gain different perspectives that will inform their writing processes.

In a way, RSS and social bookmarking are complementary digital writing tools. They both help students filter through a mass of content. RSS, because it functions as a tool to gather information and not necessarily filter it, catches everything a writer sets out to look for. Social bookmarking, on the other hand, invites the user to organize information that has already been found and share it with others, thus providing a human touch to the sorting and filtering. The ability to utilize RSS and social bookmarking together provides writers with a set of organizational tools that makes gathering information—and, in turn, writing with and about that information—more effective.

RSS (Really Simple Syndication) as a Tool for Real Writing

Really simple syndication (or rich site summary), commonly known as RSS, allows readers to subscribe to web content, just as they might choose to subscribe to a magazine and receive it at home rather than go purchase it from a store. Instead of having to visit a number of sites, web users can set up what is commonly called an aggregator or feed reader. These tools allow users to set up RSS feeds in a variety of formats and, much like an email inbox, gather all of them into one spot for easy reading. For instance, you could use any of these tools:

- Google Reader: www.google.com/reader
- Bloglines: www.bloglines.com/
- Netvibes: www.netvibes.com/
- NewsGator: www.newsgator.com/

There are two web resources that I suggest you visit before you read on, each of which will explain the concept at hand in a clear and practical manner and which, like all the other links in this text, are available as links at the book's social network (digitalwritingworkshop.ning.com/). First, the Educause Learning Initiative has created a series of papers called "7 Things You Should Know About...," available at www.educause.edu/7ThingsYouShouldKnowAboutSeries/7495. Dating back to 2005, the series offers succinct two-page PDFs that each present a pedagogical overview of a particular technology. In this case, I suggest that you go to the page for "7 Things You Should Know About RSS," available at connect.educause.edu/Library/ELI/7ThingsYouShouldKnowAbout/39401, click on the PDF, and then read to find out more about RSS. Second, consider viewing the entertaining and informative videos created by Lee and Sachi LeFever for their *Common Craft Show*, available at commoncraft.com/. Their video "RSS in Plain English," like all the others available on their site, helps explain the concept in a humorous manner; go to commoncraft.com/rss_plain_english.

Consider RSS the twenty-first-century equivalent of your mailbox and the content you receive the equivalent of a magazine. There are essentially two ways to get a magazine: go to the store and buy it or subscribe and have it delivered to your mailbox. RSS is your subscription to digital content. Once you subscribe to an RSS feed, like the magazine in your mailbox, content continues to be delivered to the reader automatically. This allows users to quickly scan news items, read blog posts, observe changes in wiki pages, listen to podcasts, and view videos, all from one interface. Many teachers are finding the capabilities of RSS very useful to help guide their own and their students' inquiry. I have also heard teachers use the term *SSR with RSS* to describe sustained silent reading with RSS. They invite their students to set up their own RSS aggregators, choose topics that are interesting to them to follow in the news and blogs, and then read those items to inspire their writing. (I explain this process in more detail later.)

Figure 2.1 shows the basic interface for my Google Reader homepage when I first log in. On the left, like many email program interfaces, basic navigation tools help guide my viewing. For this brief overview, the most important items to note are the Add Subscription button, the list of feeds shown in the lower left-hand corner (with ENG 315 in bold and feeds listed underneath in a folderlike manner), and then the main screen with the "A Look at What's New" heading. From these entry points, I am able to view the RSS feeds of numerous sources that I have gathered here, including my students' blogs, RSS feeds from other professional sources such as Edutopia (www.edutopia.org/), Google news feeds, and Google blog search feeds. For instance, I can see that

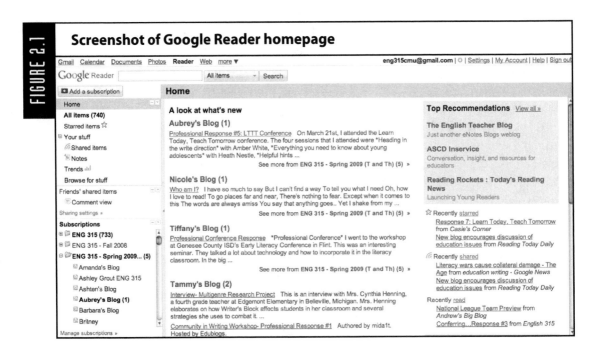

FIGURE 2.1

Screenshot of Google Reader homepage

my students, Aubrey, Nicole, Tiffany, and Tammy, have posted new items to their blogs, and that I have 740 total unread items. I can then click on any of these items and bring it up in my reader for easy viewing and, if I choose, link to the full item in its original context on the main website.

By having the content that I want and need to follow collected in one place, I have already begun my daily writing session with a collection of new links and resources that pertain directly to my own interests. This can be limiting in some respects, I know, because I am viewing only the content that I have preselected and, if I choose to follow, has links from this preselected content. As we teach students how to pursue critical inquiry and write about topics from a variety of perspectives, this could turn into a lesson about how to get a balance of content in one's aggregator so as to have a variety of materials based on the texts we read and who produces those texts. Yet, for now, I want to turn our attention back to how students can use their aggregators to discover content and pursue their own inquiry questions.

Integrating RSS into the Teaching of Writing

As teachers, we want our students to write on topics of their own choice, yet we know that they sometimes struggle to come up with ideas. By inviting them to set up an RSS aggregator, we are encouraging them to cut through some of the clutter on the Web, zeroing in on content that matters to them and can further their thinking. A number of colleagues, many involved with the National Writing Project, have set up a semester-long project in which they invite students to set up RSS readers, choose inquiry topics, and blog about those topics in a community of writers. Their public curriculum, found at youthplans .wikispaces.com/Curriculum, demonstrates the flexibility and choice that students can make in their inquiry. They ask students four essential questions:

- "What are you passionate about and how do these interests fit with our big questions?
- "What voices or sources of information do you think are important to include in your search for answers?
- "How do you become an effective networker and get people with shared interests to value your voice online?

- "How can you use our social networks as personal learning sites that lead to social action?"

Then, over the course of a semester, they invite students to subscribe to a variety of RSS feeds, including one another's blogs, and create a social network in which groups of students who share common interests are able to communicate through blog posts, photos, podcasts, and videos. In practice, this means that students spend some of their time on the computer just reading their RSS feeds, sometimes just by skimming, sometimes reading more fully. This reading can then turn into a chance to leave comments for other bloggers or on news items, or the students may pick up on an item and use it as a seed for their own blogging. No matter how they spend their time with RSS reading, the information that they receive informs their own composing practices, as they see how others are framing issues, making arguments, using examples, and embedding media such as photos, audio, and video to be digital writers.

For instance, two of my National Writing Project colleagues who are involved in the Youth Plans wiki—Paul Allison and Chris Sloan—have shared the work of their students through a weekly webcast called *Teachers Teaching Teachers*, noted in Chapter 1, and at various conferences and workshops. One particular episode, "One of the Most Moving Experiences of My Life," highlights the way in which Katie, a senior at Sloan's high school, discussed her experiences in Chicago on the evening of Barack Obama's election based on a blog post and podcast she made to their social network, Youth Voices, at youthvoices.net/ (see Figure 2.2 for the text of Katie's initial post, and see her full post as well as responses at youthvoices.net/node/2874/). One of Allison's students, Dominique, took issue with Katie's post and these two students (among many others) engaged in dialogue through the Youth Voices social network by responding to one another's posts. Before the advent of digital writing and networked spaces such as Youth Voices, this type of dialogue may have been possible in a single classroom or by doing a pen pal exchange. Yet it would have lacked the immediacy that an authentic purpose and audience can bring to the task, as evidenced in the many student comments to Katie's original post. Moreover, that audience extended well beyond Katie's classroom and, unlike a letter from a pen pal, began responding immediately. As Allison describes it,

> Being a blogger is about what young people do when they sit down to work at their computers. It is about creating a space in their lives to safely extend and explore their online voices with a group of peers, both at school, in another part of town, in another state, and around the world. The students in my classes learn about responding to each

FIGURE 2.2

"Yes We Can: My Experience in Grant Park on Election Day," by Katie Harrington.

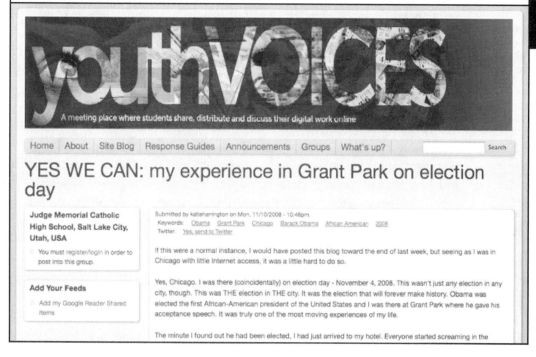

other's blogs, and how people choose to build together and share their creations and their resources. (Allison 2009, 91)

Enabling students to do this work, then, becomes part of the task of teaching in the digital writing workshop.

By engaging in their own authentic inquiry and using RSS tools to coordinate their digital writing, these students can keep track of current events through both news and blogs and can connect with other bloggers whom they can then quote, link to, and comment on, thus building their skills as active researchers and peer responders. This is a very different form of academic credibility than what we were accustomed to in our own schooling. This means that since knowledge is no longer just from the library and recorded on note cards, we must teach students to be judicious in their use of online sources. This does not mean that we should ban Wikipedia or personal blogs as sources, but it does suggest that we consider when, how, and why students might cite it as a source, or cite other blogs. Later, I explore the role of blogging in a writing workshop a bit more. Here I hypothesize just one example, and many others could be written about the hundreds of passions that our students have.

Say a student is interested in basketball. From this broad interest, he could set up news feeds for his favorite teams, subscribe to some players' blogs, and also look for other students who are interested in this topic. Now, to move him from this broad interest into something that could be used for personal writing, a teacher would ask some questions about the types of genres that he hoped to write in and, noting that students would be doing a personal essay and a research paper that term, offer some suggestions about what to look for in these RSS feeds. For instance, might this student look at how basketball players are represented in the sports and popular media? Might he look at how certain players choose social causes that they feel passionate enough about to donate time and money? These could turn into research questions. Perhaps a local charity basketball event needed publicity, and this student could blog about that organization, and the values it espoused, thus connecting some ideas for a personal essay. Through the writing workshop approach his teacher could help him meet the academic standards for quality writing as well as the expectations of particular genres while offering him the opportunity to continually pursue a topic of interest and research and write about it.

In sum, RSS works on the basis of websites sending information to you, rather than you searching for it. By subscribing to major news organizations or individual blogs, and anything else that has an RSS feed, teachers and students can gather information that is relevant to their own inquiry in a way that is sometimes more useful than by searching alone. This does not rule out Internet searching, a still critical skill. Yet in a digital writing workshop, where information continues to grow, RSS gives writers a tool to stay focused and organized while still engaging in topics that matter to them. This is a vast amount of information still, and another tool that teachers and students can use, social bookmarking, adds a personal connection to the way that information is delivered.

Social Bookmarking: Tagging and Sharing Our Interests

We all have our favorite websites. And, for most of us, links to those websites are made and stored in a folder of bookmarks or favorites in our web browsers. This is useful for us, at least if we are at the computer that holds all of our bookmarks. Social bookmarking has changed that. In a social bookmarking system, users save links to web pages that they want to remember and share. These bookmarks are usually public and can be saved privately, shared only with specified people or groups, shared only inside certain networks, and shared with another combination of public and private domains. The allowed people can usually view these bookmarks chronologically, by category or tags, or via a search engine or by subscribing to the RSS feeds of other users. Some services even allow for annotating web pages and sharing your notes with other users. Like RSS before, I encourage you to visit the Educause "7 Things You Should Know" and Common Craft Show resources on social bookmarking: net.educause.edu/ir/library/pdf/ELI7001.pdf and www.commoncraft.com/bookmarking-plain-english.

A number of social bookmarking tools exist, each with its own functionality. For instance, a few popular services include

- Diigo: www.diigo.com/
- Clipmarks: clipmarks.com/
- Delicious: delicious.com/

Each of these tools allows readers the opportunity to save a link to the URL of a site that they are reading and add to it an annotation and tags—words or phrases that describe the link and that they use to describe similar links and then access the site later from any computer that they log into with their social bookmarking account. In short, social bookmarking allows you to take your favorite websites with you.

In a digital writing workshop, then, social bookmarking can become an invaluable tool. First, because students are often moving from computer to computer in school, as well as from the library to home to their friends' computers out of school, having a centralized list of bookmarks stored in an online service makes accessing information easier. Because we want students to be good writers who cite their sources and keep good records of those sources, social bookmarking has replaced the note cards that we used to use. Second, as a teacher, you can set up your own social bookmarking account and deliver, through RSS, bookmarks to students that you find particularly interesting. The networking functions make these especially useful tools for this kind of sharing. Digital writers can quickly tag, annotate, and publicly share their bookmarks, thus making the process useful to others beyond just the initial user of the service.

Unlike traditional bookmarking, saved on our individual computers, social bookmarking is collaborative. It invites us to share our interests with one another. As a teacher, then, I could tag items for my students that would show up in their networks. Also, I can give them the URL to my social bookmarking account and invite them to subscribe to it with their RSS aggregators. Either way, as I find pertinent links, they will be able to get the links directly from me into their daily reading without having to go to a separate website, such as my school homepage, and then clicking on the links. Students, too, could set up their own networks and invite one another into conversations on their blogs about the links that they have found.

For instance, social bookmarking could become the backbone of a group inquiry project. Imagine that a group of students are all interested in photojournalism and environmental justice. Already subscribed to one another's blogs, they also each set up a social bookmarking account through Delicious and begin saving sites pertinent to these topics. They use the **for** tag to send these links to each other and soon amass a collection of dozens of websites that they are each viewing and then writing about on their blogs. Over the course of a few weeks, they begin to develop inquiry questions and go back through their list to tag sites pertinent to their final project with **project**. With the ability to sort through their tags easily to find particular websites most relevant to their project, they are able to annotate these sites with notes in the bookmark entry itself.

Over the course of time, these students are able to build personal and networked collections of bookmarks, tailored to their own inquiries. One student has a particular interest in forest habitats, while another is examining pollution in urban spaces. They both, at some point, have bookmarks that they have tagged with **trees** or **pollution**, and they can look at each other's list to get ideas about where to find more information. Like a list of topics of personal interest, this list of bookmarks serves as a fountain of ideas for helping them when they are stuck. As a part of their digital writing identities, they can quickly integrate these bookmarks into their blogs, so others who are not part of their network can see what they are interested in and, perhaps, send bookmarks their way, too. In that sense, to extend the metaphor, the fountain never runs dry when others help feed it. Finally, by keeping a digital trail of the sites that they have visited through bookmarking, these students are able to go back and cite their sources quickly without having to do time-wasting searches to find that one elusive site.

Now, with RSS and social bookmarking as a part of their lives as digital writers, students have tools that help them choose relevant topics, focus their questions for inquiry, share these resources with others, and save them for later reference. With these tools a part of their repertoire, they can begin to write about all the information that they have found through the twenty-first-century's writer's notebook: the blog.

Blogging Basics

We know that students are producing content and sharing it online through text, audio, image, and video. Research groups such as the Pew Internet and American Life Project (www.pewinternet.org/) and MacArthur digital learning initiative (digitallearning.macfound.org/) show us that, as read/write web technologies and Internet-enabled mobile phones become more popular, students continue to create blogs, social network profiles, and other online content at an increasing pace. Moreover, we know that our professional organizations such as the National Council of Teachers of English (www.ncte.org/) and the International Reading Association (www.reading.org/), among others, are calling for an increased focus on digital literacies. In our urge to incorporate new literacies in the classroom, however, we need to be mindful of what we are asking students to do. On the one hand, there certainly are dangers to creating online identities and seeking out particular information on the Web; yet, on the other hand, the Internet can provide a powerful set of tools for self-expression, as PBS' recent *Frontline* special "Growing Up Online" demonstrated (Dretzin and Maggio 2008). While some of the instances reported in this program showed youth using digital media in negative ways, one particular example demonstrated how a young woman was eventually able to use the Internet as a means of positive self-expression and identity formation.

That said, we must think carefully about how and why we want students to engage with digital writing. "[T]eachers often look for ways of fitting new technologies into classroom 'business as usual.' Since educational ends are directed by curriculum, and technologies are often regarded by teachers as 'mere' tools, the task of integrating new technologies into learning is often realized by adapting them to, or adding them onto, familiar routines" (Lankshear and Knobel 2006, 56). Rather than utilizing new technologies for newer literacies, they are instead used to complete normal academic tasks in a slightly different manner.

This mind-set essentially nullifies any experience that the students have using technologies, such as blogs, in their own ways to connect with one another and create networks. Moreover, it replicates traditional teacher-centered practices and keeps us from using the new technology in a manner that makes it a new literacy, in Lankshear and Knobel's terms. This is the "old wine in new bottles" problem (54), and it does not engage students in understanding and utilizing new literacies in productive, ethical, and responsible ways.

How, then, do we engage students in these ways with digital writing?

So far, I have discussed the ways to get students involved in their own inquiry and we know from many practitioners and researchers that students who engage in choosing their own topics and inquiry questions will be engaged in the writing process. Graves, Calkins, Atwell, and others have shown us this through their ideas about the writing workshop, and studies from the National Writing Project (2006) show that an engaged approach to teaching writing has positive outcomes on student literacy gains. We also know that students need to take those choices and questions and write about them. This writing typically begins in a writer's notebook and then moves out into the world through sharing, revision, and publication. How does this sharing, revising, and publishing happen in a twenty-first-century writing workshop? In blogs.

While the term *blog* is likely familiar, a brief definition offers insights into the technical and social aspects of blogging. According to Wikipedia:

A blog (a portmanteau of *web log*) is a website where entries are commonly displayed in reverse chronological order. "Blog" can also be used as a verb, meaning to maintain or add content to a blog. Many blogs provide commentary or news on a particular subject; others function as more personal online diaries. A typical blog combines text, images, and links to other blogs, web pages, and other media related to its topic. The ability for readers to leave comments in an interactive format is an important part of many blogs.

From a technical standpoint, then, blogs are websites that are very easy to update. From a social standpoint, they allow readers to comment easily and connect to other blogs through these comments and quoting from others' blog posts. The uses of blogs in education are many and have been written about extensively, both by edubloggers on their own blogs and through numerous books, including a few noted before in this text such as Allison, Richardson, and Warlick. As noted with RSS and social bookmarking before, I again encourage you to visit Educause and the Common Craft video series to get familiar with blogs if the explanations here are not enough: net.educause.edu/ir/library/pdf/ELI7006.pdf and www.commoncraft.com/blog.

For educators, then, blogs can serve multiple purposes. Some teachers use them to post assignments and announcements. Others use them as places for students to respond to teacher-posted prompts or to have online discussions, much like discussion forums. In a sense, this is still the "old wine in new bottles" problem. The pedagogy remains teacher centered and relies on a call-and-response model for interacting with students.

Instead, there are other possibilities. For purposes of the digital writing workshop, I consider blogs as a natural extension of the writer's notebook. Blogs maintained by individual students who are sharing and getting feedback on their own writing allow them to set up their own online presence and give and receive feedback from classmates.

There are many ways that students can blog, and each offers affordances and constraints in terms of privacy, functionality, and cost. A few of the services that many teachers and students are using now include such sites as these:

- Edublogs: edublogs.org/
- Class Blogmeister: classblogmeister.com/
- ThinkQuest: www.thinkquest.org/en/
- Ning: ning.com/

The basics of each of these platforms are the same: Students have the opportunity to log in, create blog posts, tag those posts with keywords, and then publish them. Once published, the posts are usually open to comments and are searchable through an archive. Imagine having your writer's notebook digitized and searchable.

The basics of posting to a blog can be seen in the screenshots from one of my blogs, shown in Figures 2.3 and 2.4. In this case, I am creating a post in

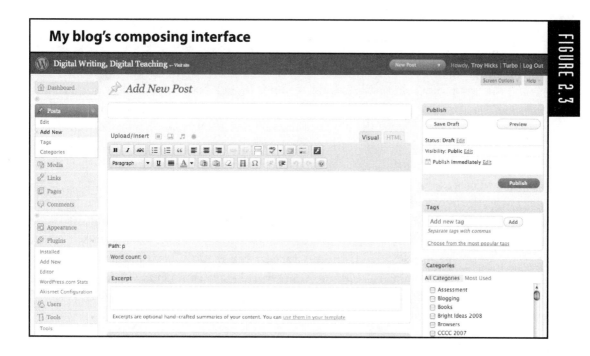

FIGURE 2.4

My blog's public interface

Digital Writing, Digital Teaching Integrating New Literacies into the Teaching of Writing

From Workshop to Classroom: The Problems of Enacting Professional Development

Troy Hicks

This past week, I was invited to present an introductory workshop on digital storytelling to a group of teachers in Alpena. Minus some minor glitches in figuring out file management with brand new jump drives, the session went well from both my perspective and that of the attendees. Exit comments were generally positive and, since I will be working with this group again, the suggestions will be very helpful, too.

Yet, in the section of the evaluations that asked teachers to rank items such as the objectives of the workshop being met, the organization, and so forth, all the positive responses were overshadowed by one question that received unusually low marks: "The impact this inservice will have on my teaching will probably be..." Responses here were at least one point lower, on average, than every other category.

This struck me as interesting because, throughout the day, we had been having discussions about access in their schools: access to computer labs and equipment, access to certain websites (such as Flickr), and access to time for planning and implementing such a project. As I reviewed these lower scores, then, I saw them not so much as a reflection on the workshop itself as much a reflection on the school contexts to which these teachers would return the next day.

I write this here not to speculate on any particular way to solve this problem, since we know the digital divide is still evident in all of our work, even in the most well endowed schools. Yet, I found it interesting that a group of engaged professionals

search

Site Host

lunarpages

Thanks to Lunar Pages, as this domain is donated as a part of their free K-12 Hosting Plan.

Copyright Info

This work is licensed under a Creative Commons Attribution-Noncommercial-Share Alike 3.0 United States License.

Site Visitors

Visitor locations

ClustrMaps   Click to see

my professional blog, Digital Writing, Digital Teaching (hickstro.org/), reflecting on a professional development session that I led about digital storytelling. Figure 2.3 shows the interface of the blog. In the main portion of the screen, the editor is present; this is where a writer composes the blog entry, and it has some of the basic functions for fonts, lists, hyperlinks, and other word-processing features. On the right, there is a list of categories that I can select from to tag the post, thus making it searchable by these tags when it shows up on my website. Once I am done writing the post, I hit the Publish button, and it shows up on my blog, as shown in Figure 2.4. Once there, it is sent through an RSS feed, and my readers can read the post in their aggregators or visit the blog to read it in context and leave comments. These technical aspects of blogs make them useful for digital writers as a new kind of writer's notebook.

Using Blogs as the New Writer's Notebook

For many teachers and students, the writer's notebook is considered a private space, and blogs, by their very nature, are quite public. That could raise eyebrows for some, yet consider that a writer can always choose to type a blog entry and keep it unpublished. Or, as mentioned earlier, the teacher could set up a private class blog with one of the services listed rather than make items available to the public Internet. No matter what the option for publishing, teachers and students should discuss the fact that anything posted online has the potential to be repurposed and distributed beyond its original point of publication, so practicing Internet safety is a must.

Hundreds, if not thousands, of teachers are using blogs with their students, for a variety of purposes. One outstanding resource for educational blogging is Steve Hargadon's wiki, SupportBlogging! (supportblogging.com/). Here, you will find links to many teachers who are bloggers themselves and inviting students to blog. Another outstanding site for student bloggers is one mentioned previously, Youth Voices (youthvoices.net/). Paul Allison, a teacher from New York City and technology liaison for the New York City Writing Project, as well as a number of his colleagues maintain these sites for their high school and middle school students. Along with these examples, take a quick browse through the thousands of sites that teachers and students blog on from the Edublogs homepage: edublogs.org/.

Blogs offer a number of distinct advantages for writers. First, along with reading and responding to other writers, the blog's author can take feedback on her own blog and use it for future posts or revisions. Second, by tagging her posts over time, the writer creates a searchable archive of posts related to a particular topic. For instance, imagine that a student is interested in dance, particularly tap and jazz. She tags all her dance-related posts with **dance**, and the specific posts with an additional tag of **tap** or **jazz**. Weeks later, she is trying to remember an idea that she used in a previous post. Rather than skim everything on her blog, she searches under the appropriate tags to find her writing. Much like a writer's notebook serves as the fertile ground for a writer's materials to grow, so does the blog, with the added benefit that it is infinitely searchable and the archives are accessible from any Internet-enabled computer. And, as Will Richardson notes, students can move from simply posting to their blogs into higher levels of thinking and academic writing by analyzing, synthesizing, and reflecting on information over time (2006, 32).

With blogs as a key component of a digital writing workshop where students can collect their writing, teachers can help individual students share their ideas with a wider audience, trace and build on their ideas over time, and present rough and final drafts of writing in an easily navigable site. Some teachers have helped their students create "blogfolios" of writing, with convenient links to the students' favorite posts that represent their thinking (creating blogfolios is further discussed in Chapter 5). Moreover, this portfolio will not get lost in the transition from grade to grade, as the student maintains ownership and can share the URL with his teacher each year.

Looking Ahead: Extending the Power of Blogging

To create and maintain blogs, two other tools can help students compose posts and keep track of their sources that they use in their posts. Both are extensions to the open-source Firefox web browser (www.mozilla.com/en-US/), a program that is free to download and install. When used in conjunction with RSS and social bookmarking to find information, these two tools can make the process of writing and citing blog posts much more efficient. The first is ScribeFire (www.scribefire.com/), a composing tool for blogging; the second is Zotero (www.zotero.org/), which is a citation manager. I offer pedagogical overviews of each tool here, as there are instructions for how to install and set up each tool on their respective websites. Both work by creating a small pop-up window in the bottom of Firefox (as shown in Figure 2.5 for Zotero) and allow you to work directly in your browser to write blog posts and manage citations.

As a composing tool, ScribeFire works much like a word processor. After configuring it to connect with your blog, you can highlight text or images on a web page and then right-click (PC) or Control+click (Mac) to bring up the contextual menu that allows you to choose ScribeFire and then Blog This Page. Once clicked, ScribeFire will open up a window in the bottom of Firefox that automatically quotes the selected material and allows for easy writing and editing of your own post by highlighting the text on the page, selecting the Blog This Page option, and then writing in the ScribeFire editor. Once you've completed your writing, you hit the Publish button and the post will go directly to your blog. ScribeFire allows you to save drafts of blog posts, add tags, and search through previously posted items, making it a useful tool for composing and revisiting digital writing.

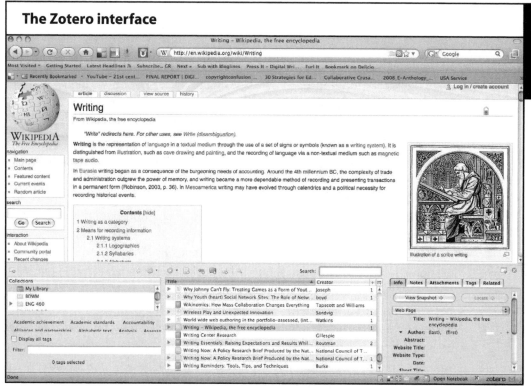

The Zotero interface

FIGURE 2.5

As a citation manager, Zotero allows you to download and manage citations for web pages, books, videos, and other online content quickly and easily. In the example shown in Figure 2.5, I have selected the page from the Wikipedia entry on "Writing" website to cite. By opening Zotero and selecting the Create New Item from Current Page option, it will save the basic bibliographic information from the website, including the URL, as in Figure 2.5. While I have found Zotero to be highly effective, it is not perfect at capturing all the information from the page, so you will need to advise students to fill out all the information needed to create a complete bibliographic record, such as the author, title, date published, and so on. Zotero can also capture information from web pages that contain bibliographic data about books such as the Library of Congress website (www.loc.gov/) or online booksellers. To get the citation for your blog post, you then right-click (PC) or Control+click (Mac) on the item in your library to bring up the contextual menu, which allows you to copy and paste it to your clipboard. This may require some toggling between ScribeFire and Zotero in the composing process, but managing multiple inputs of information is certainly a literacy skill that digital writers will need to learn.

Conclusion

We have learned from our writing workshop mentors that inquiry and choice drive the workshop approach. With RSS and social bookmarking as ways to share and gather information, students' individual choices are highly malleable, and students can easily add to and subtract from their interests. With a blog, their writing is archived and searchable, open for comments, and ready for presentation in a final portfolio. Combined, the ability to capture, share, and write about information through RSS, social bookmarking, and blogging provides students in the digital writing workshop an opportunity to write, revise, and reflect on their work in ways not possible with spiral-bound notebooks or even word-processing documents alone.

While there are some concerns about students using the Internet for collaboration—ranging from their safety to issues concerning academic integrity—there are also a number of advantages for them to use tools such as RSS, social bookmarking, and blogging, too, especially from the perspective of a writing workshop approach to teaching. Once students understand the basics of blogging, they can begin to use blogs and two additional tools of the read/write web—wikis and collaborative word processors—to engage in productive writing and conferring practices.

Conferring Through Blogs, Wikis, and Collaborative Word Processors

3

As useful as it is to teach students how to blog and keep track of online research, what we're really after is helping them compose more substantive texts, both individually and collaboratively. Such writing can occur through blogs, wikis, and collaborative word-processing tools. While offering response online is different from the face-to-face interactions that many of us find the best part of teaching writing, these types of responses allow us more time to offer substantive feedback. Moreover, many students appreciate the way in which we build relationships with them through digital writing connections. So, while it is different from our typical kinds of response, conferring with digital writing tools can be just as powerful. Bud Hunt, an edublogger and educational technologist, hints at why this happens:

> [T]here's something about the nature of the Internet, and how it functions, that helps to flesh out a vital component of the writing process that was never quite visible before. Call it connective writing, or hypertext, or what you will, but the almost tactile connections we can make between texts and folks online are dynamic and significant. There's nothing new about making text to text connections, but there's sure something powerful in the representation of those links as semi-tangible things. (Hunt 2008)

Thus, there are several ways in which others—teachers, students, and even those outside the classroom—can use blogs to offer response in the form of posting, tagging, and commenting. Students and teachers can use the basic functions of wikis to track revisions over time, specifically using a wiki's talk and history pages. Teachers and peers can also offer feedback using collaborative word processing, with specific tools for commenting and revision, and students can evaluate their own progress over time by reviewing the revisions that they have made, noting changes in both the content and form of their writing as influenced by teacher and peer comments.

The bottom line is that digital writing tools such as blogs, wikis, and collaborative word processors can enhance the writer's workshop principle of good conferring, in which we allow the writer to do most of the talking and guide him to better writing through careful questioning and feedback.

The Value of Talking with Students: What We Know About Conferring in the Writing Workshop

When Donald Murray (1985), Donald Graves (1994), and others originally endorsed talking with students about their writing, the entire field of composition shifted. Instead of relying on a model of writing instruction that attempted to perfect a student's writing, teachers began to focus on the writer herself. Over the past thirty years, we have discovered the value of conferring and its benefits, including improving relationships between the teacher and student, locating revision during a natural point of learning in the writing process, and empowering students to articulate the ebbs and flows of their own writing processes. Nancie Atwell describes it like this:

> Young writers want to be listened to. They also want honest, adult responses. They need teachers who will guide them to the meanings they don't know yet by showing them how to build on what they do know and can do. Student writers need response while the words are churning out, in the midst of the messy, tentative act of drafting meaning. And they need to be able to anticipate and predict how their teacher will approach them. (1998, 218)

Teacher response is important, as well as response from peers. As Penny Kittle believes, "Writers grow with regular response to their work and the work of other writers. Students need time to respond to each other about ideas" (2008, 85). When students use a well-defined protocol to confer with one another, they build classroom community that moves beyond the simple "Hey, it's good" type of response, and they begin to understand the ways that other writers work, thereby adding to the strategies that they might be able to use on their own. While the time we are physically able to spend with each one face-to-face limits our ability to confer with our students, we continue to promote these one-to-one meetings. Despite the challenges, the payoff is worth it for our student writers, as they gain confidence and learn new strategies in context. Lucy Calkins insists, "I've seen good teachers give up on the notion of conferring individually with their students, and this is understandable—but not acceptable. In the teaching of writing, there could be no compromise that costs so much" (1994, 223).

It is easy to feel like we have too much to cover or that conferring with individual students takes attention away from the entire class. Yet "[w]riters often talk in order to rehearse the language and content that will go into what they write, and conversation often provides an impetus or occasion for writing," as NCTE reminds us in its "Beliefs About the Teaching of Writing" (2004). How, then, might we enhance the types of talk that writers do by incorporating digital writing tools into our pedagogy; how can that facilitate the conferring we have traditionally been able to do only face-to-face?

How Digital Writing Tools Can Enhance Conferring

Why invest the precious time we have in these efforts at digital response when it could be spent planning lessons or offering holistic grades on papers? We all know that time is short, and investing time in response outside of the classroom is time spent away from these other tasks related to teaching. While it is no substitute for face-to-face response, digital responses offer a number of advantages.

First, digital response allows you time to pause and reflect on each student's needs. When we invite students to identify their needs, make those needs clear in the digital documents they produce, and then show us how they have incorporated the response that we—or their peers—have given to them, digitally capturing these responses (in text or via audio, as I suggest in the conclusion of this chapter) provide a permanence that talk during a face-to-face conference does not. This is not to say that students don't find value in face-to-face sessions; we know that they do. Yet we also know that students, like all of us, have a tendency to hear things in certain ways or, worse yet, let it go in one ear and out the other. By inserting comments directly into the document you are reading, you offer the writer a chance to go back to those comments over and over again.

Second, once the student begins revising, the digital versions of her document can be preserved automatically. We have all had a student come to us on the day that the final draft was due, saying that she failed to save a rough draft to accompany it. Perhaps that student didn't even admit this and, instead, spent a few minutes scrawling some illegible text on a crumpled piece of notebook paper, thus composing a rough draft well after the final one was complete. Or, to take the digital twist, as Jim Strickland suggests in *From Disk to Hard Copy: Teaching Writing with Computers* (1997), students can create the required outline after the document is complete (although he also maintains that this after-the-fact outlining is more helpful with revision). With blogs, writers can copy and paste their original text into new posts, tagging or naming each one as a new revision. In wikis and collaborative word processors, it is even easier. As new versions are saved, old versions are automatically archived, and the writer can go back to see changes from revision to revision, often with these changes highlighted. Unlike using stand-alone word processors that require activating an option to allow for this type of version tracking, writers don't even have to think about it when conferring through these read/write web tools.

Finally, and perhaps the most important aspect of conferring with digital writing tools, the learning doesn't have to stop at the end of workshop time. While I do not advocate that teachers make themselves available 24/7, we all know that there is never enough time during the day to reach every student in every class, even over the course of an entire week. By keeping good records of student progress in class, and using your time out of class to judiciously respond to writers who need extra help or who you were otherwise not able to see, you can continue the process of conferring online. By maintaining these relationships with your writers, as well as your understanding of what everyone is working on, you can then effectively plan whom you need to talk to the next day in class and what minilessons you need to teach.

You might ask, "Couldn't I do this with journals or writing folders?" Indeed, you could. And, many of us have, for years. Though I can't promise that the mental labor is less than the physical labor involved in toting all that paper (in fact, some teachers report that you may become more engaged in responding to student writing this way), conferring outside of class time will help accomplish all the goals just mentioned, including building relationships and responding to writers at their point of need. Moreover, when scaffolded as a part of your writing workshop, you can teach students how to respond to each other online as well, potentially increasing both the quantity and quality of responses that they may have received before only in class.

Figure 3.1 outlines some of the features that blogs, wikis, and collaborative word processors offer for individual writers, collaborative writing groups, and peer responders. As you consider the reasons for choosing a digital writing tool for a certain task, consider the affordances and constraints of the technology itself as well as the ways in which you will be asking students to share, collaborate on, or respond to work. While this figure gives a broad overview of the three types of technologies, the following sections provide more details so you can make an informed decision about how and why to use a particular digital writing tool.

Opening Up the Conversation with Blogs

Blogs, as noted in the previous chapter, offer writers an opportunity to create posts and keep an archive of their work in a single location. In a sense, the blog becomes an archive of a writer's work, easily searchable and automatically time and date stamped. By bringing the latest posts to the top of the page, and pushing older posts down on the page and, eventually, into the archive, blogs immediately highlight the writer's latest work.

As with RSS and social bookmarking (discussed in the last chapter), and with wikis and collaborative word processors (discussed in this chapter), I suggest that you return to the Educause "7 Things You Should Know About…" series and the *Common Craft* videos for information on blogs at educause.edu/ELI/7ThingsYouShouldKnowAboutBlogs/156809 and commoncraft.com/blogs, respectively, if you need to review how blogs function. While a single blog site can be authored by multiple writers (for instance, see the Students 2.0 blog at students2oh.org/), typically they are singly authored by students or, in some cases, singly authored by teachers with students posting comments on their teachers' initial posts. As noted in the last chapter, many social networks—such as the Ning created for this book, digitalwritingworkshop.ning.com/—offer built-in blogging tools, too.

In a digital writing workshop, the goal is for students to create their own blogs and connect their ideas to those of their peers. There are many ways in which teachers can create blogs, and I highlight two free ways to do so here:

FIGURE 3.1

Comparison of blogs, wikis, and collaborative word processors

	Features for Individual Writers	Features for Collaborative Writers	Features for Responders
Blogs	• Usually singly authored, although can be a part of a social network • Easily tagged and categorized by topic • Archived automatically, but revisions are not evident • Multimedia can be embedded	• The technical functions of blogs favor singly authored posts, although it is possible to save drafts of posts that multiple authors work on together • However, no easy tracking of revisions	• Comment feature is built in directly for each blog post • By using a tool such as coComment (www.cocomment.com/), responders can keep track of their comments on other blogs
Wikis	• Easy to create one's own wiki or a page within a class wiki • Page history is archived automatically, and reverting to an earlier version is easy • Multimedia can be embedded	• Individual writers can work on a page, one at a time • Revision history shows who wrote and revised the text • While writer can insert commentary in the text, it must be a different font or color	• Wiki pages have a mirror discussion page where comments can be added • Responders can view the history of a page and comment on the revisions
Collaborative Word Processors	• Files can be created in the online word processor or uploaded from computer • Basic functions of word processor evident in web browser, with output in .doc, .rtf, or other format	• Easy access for multiple writers, often available synchronously • Revision history is tracked by user • Multiple versions of document do not need to be emailed	• Full access to document for inserting comments, highlighting text, making strikeouts, and suggesting revisions, all of which can be easily changed back or deleted

first, by creating student blogs through a free service such as Edublogs (edublogs.org/) or Class Blogmeister (classblogmeister.com/), and, second, by creating a social network with built-in blogging through Ning (ning.com/). In addition, if you are looking for some more privacy and control with your students' blogging, you may want to check out, among other sites, ePals (www.epals.com/) and ThinkQuest (www.thinkquest.org/). Instead of getting hung up on all the technical aspects of signing up for these services here, I've linked to tutorials on the book's companion website (digitalwritingworkshop .ning.com/). Here, I focus on a pedagogical discussion of how and why to invite students to write with blogs.

A number of educators have been discussing blogging in recent years, and some of the more popular edubloggers include David Warlick (davidwarlick .com/2cents/), Vicki Davis (coolcatteacher.blogspot.com/), and Will Richardson (weblogg-ed.com/). Richardson suggests that there are at least eight ways to think about the types of "connective thinking" that can happen when composing a post, moving from lower levels of thinking that he defines as "not blogging" in the connective sense to higher levels that are "real" or "complex" blogging (2006, 32). For instance, to note some of the differences in the levels, students can simply post responses to journal prompts or share links. In higher levels, they can write analyses of other online materials, synthesizing across sources and building on their previous posts. No matter what the level of thinking, Richardson suggests that blogging is not the same as traditional writing in that blogging invites writers to synthesize ideas and opens up conversations between writers through commenting on the posts of others and then incorporating those posts into one's own writing. For strong examples of student blogging, return to the discussion of Youth Voices in Chapter 2 and visit that website.

In both cases, students using blogs are engaged not only in what would have been solitary writing that is, coincidentally, posted in an online space but also in digital writing where students begin reading and responding to the blogs of others. This recursive process, enabled by blogging technology, invites the same kinds of thinking that traditional face-to-face peer response does, yet demands that students read, respond, and write in ways that encourage more specific response and utilize the features of a digital writing space. That is, students who blog are able to hyperlink to sources of information and inspiration, embed multimedia for specific rhetorical purposes, and engage in larger conversations about their topic through these circles of other bloggers. Blogging, in this sense, supports the overlapping goals of increasing opportunities for students to share their work while integrating the digital literacy skills that composing with networked computers allows. As they use the comment feature to offer responses, they show that they are reading the work of others and, when offering response, metacognitively thinking about the writing process.

Students can use blogs to post all kinds of writing in a variety of genres—from works in progress to final drafts, from responses to literature to persuasive essays. When used as a writer's notebook, a blog allows students the opportunity to live what Calkins calls their "writerly lives" online, sharing their initial ideas with others and opening them up for feedback. Since this could be intimidating for some writers, we can make the processes of posting nonthreatening and perhaps allow writers who are reluctant to share their work the opportunity to simply save their items in their blog without posting them to the public portion of their blog. Showing students how you post your own writing and modeling the kinds of response that you want them to give to one another should help alleviate their fears of sharing digital writing, just as it would in traditional writing practices. As they develop their own blog posts over time and respond to their peers, they will be learning how to become better digital readers and writers, all the while enabling a writing community both inside their own classroom and potentially with students from other classrooms as well. Collaboration can happen in other ways, too; for example, wikis demonstrate the power of being able to revise and discuss one's writing as well as the writing of other students.

Collaborating and Responding with Wikis

Like blogs, wikis offer writers another way to engage in the read/write web that can support their growth over time. A wiki is a website that can be easily revised by multiple authors, and it allows for people to see the revision history as well as have a conversation about individual pages through a discussion forum. Like blogs, wikis come in different forms, and the services vary slightly from provider to provider. Wikispaces (www.wikispaces.com/) has reliable, user-friendly, ad-free spaces for K–12 educators, and I use it in my own teaching. Other popular wiki services include Wetpaint (www.wetpaint.com/), PBworks (pbworks.com/), and the former JotSpot, which has now become Google Sites (sites.google.com/). No matter which wiki you use, invite your students in with their own accounts so you can see who has made which changes to better track how they are revising.

Unlike blogs, wikis lend themselves especially well to collaborative writing for a number of reasons. Wikis are websites that can grow and develop over time, with additional pages added as a writer (or class full of writers) finds new ways to share her work. Each page on a wiki allows for features that support the act of revision, including instant editing ability in the main page, a history page that outlines the revisions the page has gone through, and a discussion page that allows for the author(s) of the page to carry on conversations with responders. Taken together, these features offer students yet another digital writing tool that can help them monitor their revision process and demonstrate growth over time. If you need to become more familiar with how wikis work, I invite you to pause in your reading and view the Educause "7 Things" text on wikis (educause.edu/ELI/7ThingsYouShouldKnowAboutWikis/156807) as well as the *Common Craft* video on them (www.commoncraft.com/video-wikis-plain-english).

To begin, the main page of a wiki acts as the public face of an ever-evolving draft. By their very nature, wikis are dynamic, subject to change at any moment. Depending on how a teacher invites his students into the use of wikis, particular pages may be kept up by individuals, small groups, or the entire class. For instance, a classroom's homepage may be seen as a space for anyone to post new content and make changes, whereas as students' individual pages are largely seen as their own spaces to share their writing. As you and your students become more comfortable with using wikis as a part of your writing community, you may choose to develop norms about how current pages get edited, future pages get added, and responders choose between editing a page itself and putting a comment on the discussion page.

Next, the history page. This component of a wiki allows the writer, or responders for that matter, the opportunity to go back and look at previously saved versions of the main wiki page. As the writer saves versions of the text, the older versions are automatically archived in this history, and different versions can be compared with one another. For instance, if the writer makes a revision to just a few words, they are typically highlighted or shown as crossed out when the two versions are compared. Over time, reflecting on these revisions could allow the writer, and responders, the opportunity to discuss the revision process in more detail, pointing out specific improvements and discussing the merits of those improvements to the overall quality of the text. Also, knowing that there is a history of changes allows the writer to make more than surface-level edits; because the old version is still there, it is easy to revert to it if a radical revision of a section of the text does not turn out as well as the writer might have hoped.

Finally, the discussion page allows for the writer and responders to carry on a conversation about the main page's text. Typically, I find that the kinds of comments most useful for students to write as well as for the writers to receive through wiki pages fall along the lines of general response (a specific model for response based on the work of the National Writing Project is offered in Chapter 5). These kinds of responses lend themselves to general reactions to the text, while inserting very specific comments and suggestions for revision seems to be better suited for when you can access the text directly, which collaborative word processors allow. In the discussion page of a wiki, all of these responses can be noted and archived, so the writer can go back and review them, even after she has made revisions to the original document.

All of these features—an easily editable main page, the history of the main page, and the discussion page—create a lively and interactive space for writers to work. Of course, one of the advantages of wikis over blogs is that collaborative writing becomes that much easier, too, since multiple writers can coauthor a single page. In addition to conferring, wikis are particularly well suited to supporting what Tori Haring-Smith (1994) calls three different types of collaborative writing. First, there is "serial writing," in which a number of individuals add small parts to a large document like a report. Then, there is "compiled writing," in which writers add their own individual pieces into a collection, such as an anthology of poems. Finally, "coauthored writing" blends the work of many writers into a unified voice. Depending on your goal for a particular assignment as well as what you want individual writers to accomplish, any of these three forms of collaborative writing could be a useful way for students to use a wiki to its full potential as a collective working space.

Moving our students from peer conferrers to collaborators is challenging. Based on conversations with colleagues and my own personal experience, I offer a few suggestions for how to open up students to the differences between just helping someone else and truly collaborating with him. Based on a presentation at a National Writing Project meeting that I facilitated with Peter Kittle (2006), the group developed this list of ideas for how to engage students in constructive collaboration:

- Open up discussion about ethical concerns related to individual authorship and one's responsibility to the group.
- Let students mess up documents and then fix them (revert to previous versions).
- Make the social behaviors of collaboration (e.g., listening, asking open-ended questions, repeating ideas heard from others) transparent.

- Have each individual name her assets and liabilities as a group member and choose tasks for writing accordingly.
- Create a list of specific steps for the group and individuals to take.
- Have frank discussions about the nature of revision—especially how some of the first-draft writing will be cut or significantly changed—so no one gets offended.
- Examine and acknowledge changing group dynamics.
- Encourage participants to ask good questions and keep conversations going by moving beyond simple responses to writing and into deeper discussions about revision.

Once you have engaged students in this conversation, you can have them begin collaborative writing with a wiki. Along with perusing the lesson idea presented in the appendix, "Exploring Copyright Through Collaborative Wiki Writing," visit the following sites for some other examples of how teachers and students are using wikis:

- Educational Wikis (educationalwikis.wikispaces.com/) and Best Education Wikis (www.wetpaint.com/category/Education): Each of these pages offers general lists of wikis that educators have created and are using in a variety of ways.
- Terry the Tennis Ball (terrythetennisball.wikispaces.com/): Students from Mr. Pearce's grades 3–4 class at Bellaire Primary School in Geelong, Victoria, Australia, wrote collaboratively about the adventures of a tennis ball named Terry, much in the style of a "choose your own adventure" story. Each page ends with two or more hyperlinks for the reader to choose from, each representing an action that will happen to Terry, and students continue to develop new pages for the adventure.
- Kabodian7 (kabodian7.pbworks.com/): Aram Kabodian, a seventh-grade English language arts teacher at MacDonald Middle School in East Lansing, Michigan, and technology liaison for the Red Cedar Writing Project, has set up this wiki for his class, using it as a hub for everything from daily assignments to a space for students to post their work, including digital videos created as public service announcements.

In another instance, I helped a colleague set up a wiki for a young adult literature class in which her students were able to develop pages for individual books and authors, posting summaries of the texts they had read for class and carrying on conversations about characters, plot, setting, theme, and other story elements on the wiki's discussion pages. In my own writing methods class, students post their work and receive comments from their peers, but rarely do they revise one another's words (eng315.wikispaces.com). No matter what the use for wikis, their point is to encourage collaboration, and so long as you are explicit about the kinds of collaboration you expect from your students, they will likely rise to that expectation and work together to write and confer in ways they could not have done without the options a wiki provides them. Another tool to aid in their growth as digital writers, collaborative word processors, can push them in additional directions.

Engaging in Deep Revision with Collaborative Word Processors

Moving students from conferring to revising remains a constant challenge for any teacher. Meredith Sue Willis describes the great rewards revision can bring writers, in terms of both the process and the final product:

> To grow accustomed to making changes and working one's way back into a piece is to be well on the way to serious, deep revision.... Children, like adult writers, want their work to be treated with interest and respect, to be shared with others and enjoyed, but a child in a supportive classroom with an appreciative teacher learns that making changes can be a positive experience, even fun: you can add things, take away things, make a second draft, get ideas from a partner, turn a description into a story, turn a story into a play, turn a play into an opera. It is atmosphere and attitude that count here. (1993, 2)

When students are able to confer with their teacher and their peers, over time and on a variety of texts, they can move toward the kind of deep revision described by Willis. Using collaborative word processors as a tool for drafting, revising, and getting response to their writing allows students a number of advantages that can move them quickly toward deep revision. Again, Educause outlines a number of these points in a clear and succinct manner in its "7 Things" piece on collaborative editing (educause.edu/ELI/7ThingsYouShould KnowAboutColla/156812), and you can view the *Common Craft* video on Google Docs (www.commoncraft.com/video-googledocs) to get a short and simple explanation. There are a number of online, collaborative word processors that you could invite students to use. For instance, Sean Aune (2008) outlines thirteen different ones, including two that I use often: Google Docs and Zoho Writer. For our purposes, I focus on the use of Google Docs here, although I invite you to explore the benefits of a few different word processors before deciding what is best for you and your students.

First, with networked computers, it is simple to upload and share documents using collaborative word processors, be it at home, school, the library, or a friend's or relative's home. More importantly, these documents are easy for students to share with collaborators, including you and their peers. By going to one main website, such as docs.google.com/, and logging in with a user name and password, students can gain access to all their documents, as well as all the documents others have shared with them. I cannot overemphasize the advantage of this kind of access. While it is true that some students may still face the digital divide in their schools, homes, and communities, the idea that they can access their documents on any networked computer at any time without transferring the files or having to worry about file conversion is, quite simply, groundbreaking for us as educators. No lost files on the network or at home. No emails. No compatibility issues. Just quick and easy access for our students to share their writing with us and each other.

Second, students and teachers can offer feedback in a variety of ways, including inserting comments, striking through text, changing font color, and highlighting text with collaborative word processors. All of these methods invite you into the students' text and offer you the opportunity to give very specific feedback in terms of editing or more substantive revisions. Two cautions here: Beware of turning these tools into the digital equivalent of a red pen. This is not to say that we should avoid being direct with students; it is to say that we need to encourage them to keep ownership of their own writing and that our comments should be constructive for them as writers, not just focused only on revising a particular section of writing (or, worse yet, revising it for them). Second, when offering feedback, be judicious. My experience tells me that middle and high school students typically focus on one big idea during revision, and they can track one or two patterns of error. In other words, even though the digital tools make it easier to point out revisions and errors, be sure to stay focused in your feedback.

The third, and perhaps most important, benefit of collaborative word processors is they allow the writer and the responder to track the revision history of the text quickly and easily. Like wikis, collaborative word processors track the versions of the document automatically each time it is saved. These versions—whether simply showing an added comma or an entirely revised paragraph—are all archived as a part of the document's history. No more students going back to their seats to quickly scribble out a "rough draft" of the paper they're about to hand in to you. Now you can invite students to use the different saved versions to write commentaries on their revision process, focusing on particular sections of the text and copying and pasting the different versions of those sections into their commentary for elaboration.

While blogs, wikis, and collaborative word processors do offer a number of advantages, there are disadvantages to consider when incorporating them into your writing workshop. First, there is always the caution that you could have your students spread themselves across so many digital writing spaces that they become either confused about or ambivalent to using the particular tools. For instance, beginning one's work on a blog and then having to copy and paste it to a wiki or a collaborative word processor takes time and spreads the same writing into different locations. Figuring out which draft is where could be time-consuming as students work on multiple pieces. Another disadvantage comes from the fact that students will need to have accounts with the various web-based services you use for digital writing. Even after getting the appropriate permissions and acceptable use policies for students to use these tools, teaching them strategies for creating account names and managing passwords can be a time-consuming and frustrating experience. No teacher wants to hear the newest version of the dog eating a student's homework: "I forgot my password!"

That said, I hope that you see the power collaborative word processors can offer the revision process. To make this point even more clear, I offer an example from Heather Lewis, middle school language arts teacher and Red Cedar Writing Project teacher consultant, as well as a sample of the letter that she sends home to parents about why she wants students to be able to work in Google Docs (see Figure 3.2).

In the two screenshots shown in Figures 3.3 and 3.4, you can see the revision history for this student's writing, both in the final form in Figure 3.3 as well as with Google Docs' revision history turned on in Figure 3.4. While Figure 3.3 shows the final version of the document, with identifying information from the student and point totals removed for privacy, you can see Heather Lewis' comments in the document that helped guide revision. Figure 3.4 is where the action took place, showing how her student revised by adding some details and moving major sections of the text in order to better meet the requirements of the assignment. Imagine this revision process playing out in dozens of your students' writing pieces, every day, and how tracking these changes would allow them to reflect on their growth as writers over time.

FIGURE 3.2

Sample permission letter for use of Google Docs

September 2008

Waverly Middle School
Mrs. Lewis
English 8

Dear Parent/Guardian:

GoogleApps is a free Internet site that allows users to have access to programs very similar to Microsoft Word, Excel, and PowerPoint. People can save these documents on the Internet and access them anywhere there is a computer and an Internet connection. In addition, once someone creates, for example, a document, he or she can share this document with other people logged into GoogleDocs. Multiple people can view and revise a piece of writing. This not only allows collaboration but also gives the students access to their work wherever there is the Internet.

My class will be using this program, creating pieces of writing, inviting friends and myself to view and help with revision of their documents. Ultimately, I will grade their papers with this technology.

The sign-up process will be done in the computer lab at school. However, I will have to create a Gmail account for each student so they each can have access to GoogleDocs. I will explain that this email is to be used *only* for the purposes of our classroom. Their user name and password will be the same as the school login for them and they are *not* allowed to change them. Please let me know if you have any concerns in this endeavor. It will be an educational experience in learning about new technology, social networking, and revision in writing as a process that met much success last year.

Please see this site for more information: docs.google.com/.

Heather Lewis

Looking Ahead: Responding with Voice, Literally

In addition to the previously discussed ways that we can share our responses to our students' texts, there is one other strategy that we can begin to consider: sharing our voices, literally, with students through digital audio recordings. I have heard anecdotes of teachers who would record comments on a cassette

FIGURE 3.3

Final version of student writing in Google Docs

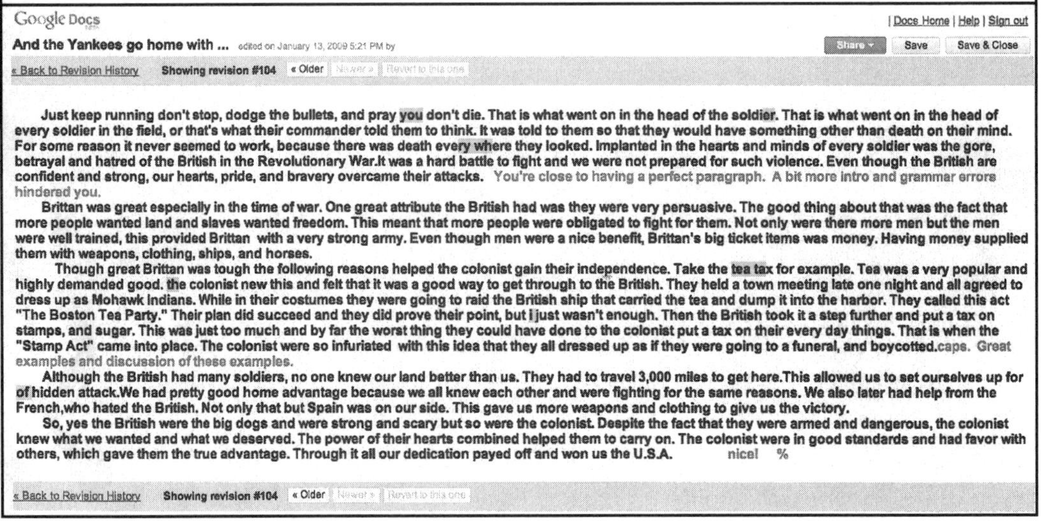

Google Docs | Docs Home | Help | Sign out

And the Yankees go home with ... edited on January 13, 2009 5:21 PM by

Share ▾ | Save | Save & Close

« Back to Revision History **Showing revision #104** « Older | Newer » | Revert to this one

Just keep running don't stop, dodge the bullets, and pray you don't die. That is what went on in the head of the soldier. That is what went on in the head of every soldier in the field, or that's what their commander told them to think. It was told to them so that they would have something other than death on their mind. For some reason it never seemed to work, because there was death every where they looked. Implanted in the hearts and minds of every soldier was the gore, betrayal and hatred of the British in the Revolutionary War.It was a hard battle to fight and we were not prepared for such violence. Even though the British are confident and strong, our hearts, pride, and bravery overcame their attacks. You're close to having a perfect paragraph. A bit more intro and grammar errors hindered you.

Brittan was great especially in the time of war. One great attribute the British had was they were very persuasive. The good thing about that was the fact that more people wanted land and slaves wanted freedom. This meant that more people were obligated to fight for them. Not only were there more men but the men were well trained, this provided Brittan with a very strong army. Even though men were a nice benefit, Brittan's big ticket items was money. Having money supplied them with weapons, clothing, ships, and horses.

Though great Brittan was tough the following reasons helped the colonist gain their independence. Take the tea tax for example. Tea was a very popular and highly demanded good. the colonist new this and felt that it was a good way to get through to the British. They held a town meeting late one night and all agreed to dress up as Mohawk Indians. While in their costumes they were going to raid the British ship that carried the tea and dump it into the harbor. They called this act "The Boston Tea Party." Their plan did succeed and they did prove their point, but i just wasn't enough. Then the British took it a step further and put a tax on stamps, and sugar. This was just too much and by far the worst thing they could have done to the colonist put a tax on their every day things. That is when the "Stamp Act" came into place. The colonist were so infuriated with this idea that they all dressed up as if they were going to a funeral, and boycotted.caps. Great examples and discussion of these examples.

Although the British had many soldiers, no one knew our land better than us. They had to travel 3,000 miles to get here.This allowed us to set ourselves up for of hidden attack.We had pretty good home advantage because we all knew each other and were fighting for the same reasons. We also later had help from the French,who hated the British. Not only that but Spain was on our side. This gave us more weapons and clothing to give us the victory.

So, yes the British were the big dogs and were strong and scary but so were the colonist. Despite the fact that they were armed and dangerous, the colonist knew what we wanted and what we deserved. The power of their hearts combined helped them to carry on. The colonist were in good standards and had favor with others, which gave them the true advantage. Through it all our dedication payed off and won us the U.S.A. nice! %

« Back to Revision History **Showing revision #104** « Older | Newer » | Revert to this one

FIGURE 3.4

Final version of student writing showing revision history in Google Docs

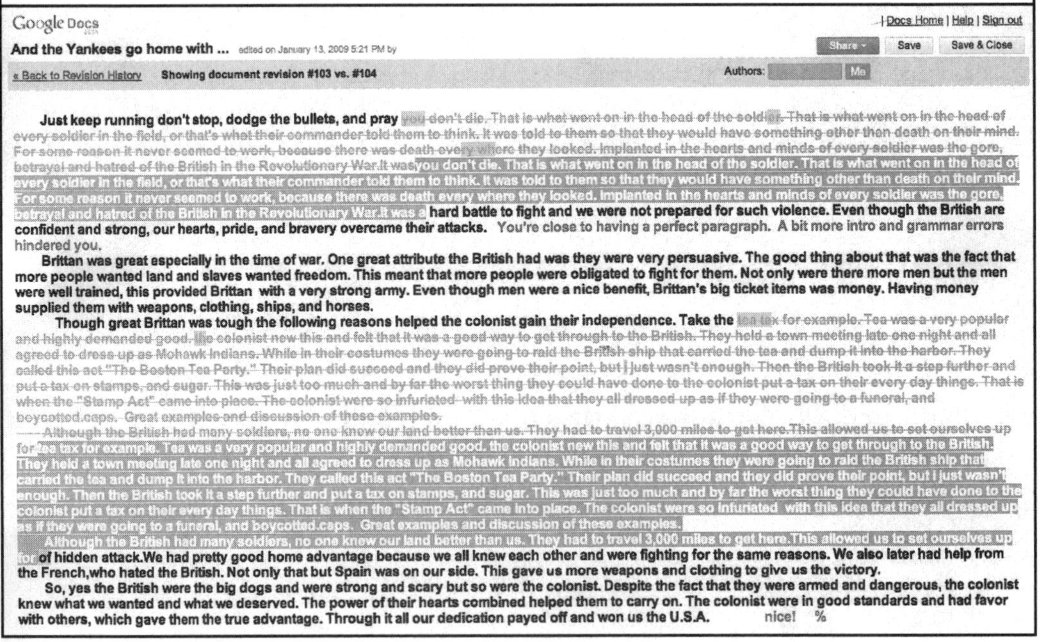

Google Docs | Docs Home | Help | Sign out

And the Yankees go home with ... edited on January 13, 2009 5:21 PM by

Share ▾ | Save | Save & Close

« Back to Revision History **Showing document revision #103 vs. #104** Authors: Me

Just keep running don't stop, dodge the bullets, and pray ~~you don't die. That is what went on in the head of the soldier. That is what went on in the head of every soldier in the field, or that's what their commander told them to think. It was told to them so that they would have something other than death on their mind. For some reason it never seemed to work, because there was death every where they looked. Implanted in the hearts and minds of every soldier was the gore, betrayal and hatred of the British in the Revolutionary War.It was~~ you don't die. That is what went on in the head of the soldier. That is what went on in the head of every soldier in the field, or that's what their commander told them to think. It was told to them so that they would have something other than death on their mind. For some reason it never seemed to work, because there was death every where they looked. Implanted in the hearts and minds of every soldier was the gore, betrayal and hatred of the British in the Revolutionary War.It was a hard battle to fight and we were not prepared for such violence. Even though the British are confident and strong, our hearts, pride, and bravery overcame their attacks. You're close to having a perfect paragraph. A bit more intro and grammar errors hindered you.

Brittan was great especially in the time of war. One great attribute the British had was they were very persuasive. The good thing about that was the fact that more people wanted land and slaves wanted freedom. This meant that more people were obligated to fight for them. Not only were there more men but the men were well trained, this provided Brittan with a very strong army. Even though men were a nice benefit, Brittan's big ticket items was money. Having money supplied them with weapons, clothing, ships, and horses.

Though great Brittan was tough the following reasons helped the colonist gain their independence. Take the ~~tea tax for example. Tea was a very popular and highly demanded good. the colonist new this and felt that it was a good way to get through to the British. They held a town meeting late one night and all agreed to dress up as Mohawk Indians. While in their costumes they were going to raid the British ship that carried the tea and dump it into the harbor. They called this act "The Boston Tea Party." Their plan did succeed and they did prove their point, but i just wasn't enough. Then the British took it a step further and put a tax on stamps, and sugar. This was just too much and by far the worst thing they could have done to the colonist put a tax on their every day things. That is when the "Stamp Act" came into place. The colonist were so infuriated with this idea that they all dressed up as if they were going to a funeral, and boycotted.caps. Great examples and discussion of these examples.~~

~~Although the British had many soldiers, no one knew our land better than us. They had to travel 3,000 miles to get here.This allowed us to set ourselves up for~~ tea tax for example. Tea was a very popular and highly demanded good. the colonist new this and felt that it was a good way to get through to the British. They held a town meeting late one night and all agreed to dress up as Mohawk Indians. While in their costumes they were going to raid the British ship that carried the tea and dump it into the harbor. They called this act "The Boston Tea Party." Their plan did succeed and they did prove their point, but i just wasn't enough. Then the British took it a step further and put a tax on stamps, and sugar. This was just too much and by far the worst thing they could have done to the colonist put a tax on their every day things. That is when the "Stamp Act" came into place. The colonist were so infuriated with this idea that they all dressed up as if they were going to a funeral, and boycotted.caps. Great examples and discussion of these examples.

Although the British had many soldiers, no one knew our land better than us. They had to travel 3,000 miles to get here.This allowed us to set ourselves up for of hidden attack.We had pretty good home advantage because we all knew each other and were fighting for the same reasons. We also later had help from the French,who hated the British. Not only that but Spain was on our side. This gave us more weapons and clothing to give us the victory.

So, yes the British were the big dogs and were strong and scary but so were the colonist. Despite the fact that they were armed and dangerous, the colonist knew what we wanted and what we deserved. The power of their hearts combined helped them to carry on. The colonist were in good standards and had favor with others, which gave them the true advantage. Through it all our dedication payed off and won us the U.S.A. nice! %

tape for their students, rather than write marginal notes, adding to the tape as subsequent drafts and new assignments were completed. Melissa Pomerantz (2008), a high school English teacher in St. Louis, Missouri, responds to hundreds of student papers each semester using digital audio, and her students report their enjoyment at having this virtual conversation with her. With simple, free tools like Audacity (audacity.sourceforge.net/), we now have the possibility of recording audio and easily sharing it with students via email. For a review of Audacity, I suggest you take a look at the screencasts created by my National Writing Project colleague Chris Sloan (www.judgememorial.com/sloan/audacity/). When I have recorded and shared a response to my students through this method, they told me that, after the initial shock of hearing their teacher's disconnected voice coming through their computer, they appreciated hearing me talking directly to them rather than reading comments on a rubric. I am able to be very direct with each student and, often, I am able to respond more quickly in an audio recording than I would have if I'd had to type out that much information.

There are concerns with this practice, of course. First, an unscrupulous student could take your audio file and post it publicly online or otherwise remix it and use it for nefarious purposes. To my knowledge, none of my students have done this, yet I try to protect myself in some sense by never stating a grade in these types of responses and choosing my words carefully when critiquing certain parts of a student's text. Even though you are speaking, and have the advantage of tone and inflection to make your points, you are not sitting right next to a student in a face-to-face conference, so being sensitive to how your student will be listening to this recording is important. In short, I suggest that you imagine that you are sitting with the student, engaged in a conference, but that your conference is being recorded and could someday be used, for better or for worse, as an example of how to confer with students.

Taken together, the opportunities that blogs, wikis, collaborative word processors, and even recorded responses offer to you as you confer with student writers are numerous. While students are able to track their own revisions and directly comment on the ways in which they have incorporated your responses, there are no more lost disks or postdated rough drafts. These features allow for more comprehensive conferring and deeper reflection, thus encouraging our students to engage more fully in their writing, both during our workshop time in school as well as for their own purposes outside of school.

Examining Author's Craft Through Multimedia Composition

As a staple of writing workshop pedagogy, examining author's craft can be made more powerful by writing with multimedia. Return, for a moment, to the image in Chapter 1 of Aram Kabodian's students writing their PSA in the form of a digital video. What elements of craft do they need to be aware of and be able to transfer from their understanding of print texts? For instance, what makes a good introduction—does it involve text, an image, music, narration, or some combination of these? What kind of details are necessary to make the point of the PSA clear, and how does a digital writer align transitions from idea to idea in terms of transitioning from screen to screen? For instance, is fading to black more useful than a sliding screen? What makes the biggest impact for a conclusion? In all these elements of craft, there are a number of decisions to make, oftentimes interrelated decisions that require writers to make careful choices about the ways in which text, image, video, and audio are combined to deliver an overall message.

To consider these questions, I turn to a point that Kathleen Blake Yancey made in her 2008 presidential address at the annual convention of the National Council of Teachers of English. In her talk, Yancey encouraged us to not think of students merely as writers, but instead think of them as composers. Multimedia authoring requires students to combine text, images, audio, and video in ways that rely on our traditional understandings of what it means to create good writing, but the situation is vastly different. Sometimes a picture—or an audio clip of a speaker, or a sound effect, or a few seconds of video—is worth a thousand words, ones that do not necessarily need to be written. We still need to teach craft, and our students certainly need to understand it to make effective multimedia texts, yet the tone of our conversation needs to shift in order to accommodate how digital writers compose.

To step back for a moment and consider how and why we look at these craft elements of writing, I first have to make a distinction. From my perspective there are two ways to consider examining author's craft by using digital writing tools: first, by utilizing digital tools to examine author's craft from print-based writing and, second, by examining the craft of multimedia composition in the way that Yancey and others have described it, such as Anne Frances Wysocki, who argues that "new media needs to be informed by what writing teachers know, precisely because writing teachers focus specifically on texts and how situated people (learn how to) use them to make things happen" (Wysocki 2004, 5). When looking at author's craft from print-based texts with digital tools, there is no doubt that the tools can be useful. From the first perspective, then, all the elements of craft such as leads, conclusions, adding details, and inserting dialogue can be enhanced with these digital writing tools. For instance, students can manipulate text with word processors in ways that allow them to easily revise sentences for fluency, try out different words with a built-in thesaurus, and sample different text patterns by copying an author's words and then mimicking the sentence's pattern. I invite and encourage you to use the tools discussed in the previous chapter—blogs, wikis, and collaborative word processors—to share your own writing as well as small excerpts from the writing of others, from published authors to fellow students, and then look at craft using the tools available. Whether students are highlighting words and inserting comments with the word processor or putting comments on a blog post or wiki page, exploring craft using these digital tools can make the process more engaging for all the reasons previously discussed.

That said, I have taken the second perspective when speaking of author's craft in this chapter. I take the principles of craft that we use when creating print texts, such as leads and conclusions, but focus on multimedia composition. Writing with new media—such as the examples in this chapter of photo-essays, podcasts, and digital stories or videos—offers students opportunities to think about traditional elements of author's craft and create additional chances for image, audio, and video to be layered into the digital writing process. Some discussions about craft will sound very similar from print to multimedia environments; for instance, what details are appropriate and useful in this text so my point is clear? Yet others are new and distinctly different; for instance, how does one compose, collect, and organize images for a photo-essay? What considerations need to be taken into account in terms of the technologies used and the audiences reached?

By examining author's craft through the lens of newer literacies, then, we will explore how to encourage student writers to use elements of author's craft while composing multimedia texts. As we continue to examine how and why digital writers compose these texts, keeping in mind the fundamental principles of author's craft that have been articulated by teachers and researchers, such as Ralph Fletcher and JoAnn Portalupi (1998) and Barry Lane (1992, 1999), will help us guide our students in making informed choices as digital writers.

Understanding Author's Craft in a Digital Age

As a key component of the writing workshop, craft lessons invite students into the writing process by allowing teachers opportunities to discuss the ways that authors construct texts. Teachers devote time in minilessons and conferences to examining the ways that authors literally craft their work; that is, how do they construct engaging leads, create depth in characters through dialogue, and engage readers through thoughtful repetition of a word or phrase, for example? Looking at craft in this way, the place where Fletcher and Portalupi call "the cauldron in which the writing gets forged" (1998, 3), allows students to see what good writers do as well as how they do it. That is, if we simply advise students to "show, don't tell," we miss out on actually demonstrating for students how to read like writers through the teaching of craft. By doing so, we could be giving them new insights into how good authors create texts, elements of author's craft they can emulate in their own writing. "Show, don't tell," of course, takes on new meaning in multimedia writing and gives us even more opportunities to discuss how written text, images, audio, and video can work together to create a more powerful composition.

Given this understanding of author's craft, we also realize that the composing process for new media changes things. A lot. Writing multimedia texts both honors our traditional understanding of what good writing is while at the same time offers us new definitions of what makes, to reiterate the previous examples, a compelling lead, effective characterizations, and successful use of repetition for rhetorical effect. The elements of author's craft in new media writing can be seen as a combination of how filmmakers, photographers, radio producers, musicians, website designers, and, of course, writers think about getting their points across in a chosen medium.

As noted earlier, while I am not intentionally ignoring the tools that we learned about in Chapter 3—blogs, wikis, and collaborative word processors—I see these tools as opportunities for networked writing that is still, primarily, text based. Adding images, hyperlinks, and other elements of multimedia production can and do cause us to rethink how these tools are used. Yet these types of digital writing tools still rely heavily on the physical act of writing—typing into the computer letters that form words, sentences, paragraphs, and, eventually, entire pieces. I don't want to underestimate how using these particular technologies can help us explore craft, or how writing itself is critical to the production of multimedia texts through brainstorming and storyboarding; yet that is not the focus for this chapter. Instead, we need to turn our attention to the kinds of digital writing that are combining text, images, sounds, and other media elements into single texts such as digital photo-essays, podcasts, and digital stories.

By stretching your thinking into new media compositions, you can take advantage of new ways to examine author's craft with your students. Before discussing these specific technologies, however, I want to introduce a heuristic, a tool that you can share with your students to think about the elements of author's craft, especially in new media writing. You can teach students to apply this heuristic to various types of multimedia writing, such as digital photo-essays, podcasts, and digital stories, articulating questions of craft that can guide your digital writers as they compose these texts.

Reading the "MAPS" to Examine Author's Craft

As outlined by Swenson and Mitchell (2006), there is a simple acronym that offers teachers a heuristic to help students think critically about the texts they are reading and writing: MAPS. The original acronym was built from *mode*, *audience*, *purpose*, and *situation*, both for the writer as an individual as well as the context of the writing; I add a second *M* to this heuristic: *media*. Like Gunther Kress and Theo Van Leeuwen (2001), I make the distinction between the mode (or, to use a synonym more common to writing teachers, genre) of a particular text and media (that is, according to Kress and Van Leeuwen, "the tools and the materials" used to create a particular text) (22). For instance, a writer can compose in the mode of a memoir or, as in the following example, a persuasive text, yet present that memoir or persuasive text through different media, such as a digital movie or podcast. A digital writer constantly questions the ways in which a text is being produced—from the purpose and audience to whom she is writing, to the choice of technologies used to compose a text, to how that text is distributed—and MAPS helps writers make those decisions.

Digital writers must make rhetorical choices about how to craft their texts based on their own writing skills, the tools and digital resources they have available, the time allotted for the task, and a number of other factors. Thus, Figure 4.1 outlines these aspects of the MAPS heuristic—mode and media, audience, purpose, and situation for the writing and of the writing itself—explaining each one, and then offers a comparison of the MAPS for writing a traditional persuasive essay as compared with composing a digital video that takes the form of a public service announcement. I chose these two types of texts since, in essence, they have the same purpose: to move someone into action. Yet, in many other senses, they are quite different and present a number of choices for digital writers who are trying to utilize elements of author's craft to make their points. And, if it helps, return again to the image in Chapter 1 of students composing their PSA and think about how the process in which they are engaged is similar to and different from what they would be doing if writing a persuasive essay.

While it is, perhaps, quite obvious that writing a persuasive essay and creating a PSA as a video have similar aims but are very different processes, the MAPS heuristic helps articulate those differences (and, in some sense, it shows how the similarities can help inform one's writing process). As this brief sample shows, examining the MAPS of a particular piece of writing allows us to think about how a text is structured, the knowledge and skills that a writer needs to construct such a text, and how the affordances and constraints of a particular mode and medium allow a writer to communicate his ideas. While it is not inherently easy for any of us to write a persuasive essay, it is certainly a mode and medium that is emphasized across a student's K–12 career, especially in the secondary years, to a point that it becomes second nature to write one. Thus, the skills a writer needs to craft such an essay—the ability to identify a topic, take a stand, gather evidence, compose an outline that becomes an essay, and finally revise and edit—are a part of the culture of writing in K–12 curricula and classrooms. For a thorough list of academic vocabulary that can enhance your descriptions of the modes in and purposes for which we ask

The MAPS heuristic

FIGURE 4.1

	Explanation	Example 1: Print-Based Persuasive Essay	Example 2: Public Service Announcement Video
Mode	*Mode* generally refers to the genre of the text, an essay, for instance; specifically, it helps us differentiate between particular subgenres such as a persuasive essay and an expository essay.	Here, the mode of a text-based persuasive essay typically requires a thesis statement that is supported with appropriate details and examples; page length can vary, but the "five paragraph" theme is a typical model.	In this case, a PSA generally must fit in a thirty- or sixty-second format suitable for showing on TV or the Web; the message must be clear and concise, typically with a slogan used for effect.
Media	*Media* refers to the way in which the text is presented: for instance, different media are used when creating a standard word-processed text, a trifold brochure on glossy paper, and a digital story with images and narration.	Essays can begin with handwritten notes and are typically composed with word processors. While some use of charts or images may be appropriate, the final product generally is completed as a print document with minimal use of visuals.	Begun on paper with a storyboard, the final product takes the form of a digital video that can be distributed in multiple formats including broadcast TV, DVD, CD-ROM, or web-based video-sharing sites.
Audience	*Audience* refers to the characteristics of those who are most likely to receive your work and what they value in good writing; the difference in expectations between writing an email to a friend as compared with your supervisor, for instance.	While persuasive essays can be written to any audience, and there are many examples of students writing beyond the classroom walls and having an impact on their communities, essays are typically turned in to the teacher for final grading.	By nature of the media, PSAs are meant to be distributed to wider audiences as well as for evaluation in the classroom. Distribution might come from a public performance of the work at the school level or through sharing the video by the media noted above.

(continues)

FIGURE 4.1

The MAPS heuristic (continued)

	Explanation	Example 1: Print-Based Persuasive Essay	Example 2: Public Service Announcement Video
Purpose	*Purpose* refers to the specific action that a writer aims to accomplish with a piece; more than just persuade, for instance, will the piece try to politely influence or thoroughly convince the reader?	In this case, purpose is tied closely to the mode and media in that academic audiences expect texts to be thesis driven and well supported. Thus, the purpose must be made entirely clear early on in the paper in the form of a thesis statement.	By incorporating words, images, video, music, and narration, the writer does not necessarily have to make a clear written statement of purpose in the video. Through the combined effect of multimedia, the purpose can be more implicit than overt.
Situation for the Writer	As writers, we each have particular strengths and weaknesses in terms of our work habits; this ranges from the genres we prefer to write in, to the type of environment we create for writing, to the technologies that we are comfortable composing with.	As writers, our students are exposed to this formal type of writing early in their academic careers. Many recognize the patterns of a thesis-driven essay, even if they are not all able to replicate the pattern in their own writing.	Having been exposed to PSAs in a variety of media—print, audio, and video—students are familiar with the genre, even if they are unfamiliar with the actual skills related to producing a digital video. Commercials, in short, are a part of our culture that students understand.
Situation of the Writing	Particular writing tasks make demands of us, too; deadlines, genre expectations, the implementation of new media such as audio or video, and those with whom we are collaborating can all influence how well we work.	As a standard form of academic writing, the persuasive essay has currency among teachers of writing and is, unfortunately, sometimes conceived of in formulaic ways. Writers must meet these expectations while still attempting to be original with their thesis and supporting details.	Requiring the use of a personal computer, digital video camera, and perhaps other technologies, the digital video demands additional hardware, software, and skills beyond what is typically needed for creating a document with a word processor.

students to write, see pages 179–80 in Jim Burke's *Writing Reminders: Tools, Tips, and Techniques* (2003).

One could ask why, if the persuasive essay is so valued in school, should we worry about teaching students the rhetorical and technical aspects of creating a PSA? While some courses such as media production may focus on these skills, the shift toward seeing these skills as embedded in the work of writing teachers is becoming more and more prevalent. The trick, of course, is not to see these additional modes and media as ones that we have to add on to the writing that we already invite students to do. Instead, we need to conceive of them as alternative or supplemental ways of meeting the goals that have been long set in the writing curriculum. As numerous teachers and scholars have argued, and I have tried to articulate throughout this book, all writing is informed by these newer, multiple, and digital literacies. There is simply no question that students are influenced by a variety of texts that they encounter in the world, and learning how to compose in multimedia environments is a critical skill, and not just because the curriculum guidelines suggest it is so.

As a writer, a composer, I need to think about all these different elements in MAPS, and these help me figure out the moves that I am allowed to make with a given composition. Moreover, the heuristic helps me consider what moves are desirable to make, too. It helps in the decision-making process as a writer thinks about the composing task, the tools and resources available, the time allotted, and the final goals for the project. And, as outlined briefly in the next section, these metacognitive skills are becoming more and more a part of what it means to be a writer in a digital age.

Looking at Standards for Digital Learning

To further articulate this point about why we should teach students to compose in multimedia environments, a number of policy briefs, reports, and curriculum documents from state departments of education and professional organizations such as the National Council of Teachers of English (NCTE) and the International Society for Technology Education (ISTE) outline many technical skills and personal dispositions that students should have in order to be digitally literate, twenty-first-century citizens. While there are many points that could be made from these documents (they are discussed more in Chapter 6 in relation to assessment) I highlight only one item from each of these documents for sake of example, and encourage you to examine them in more detail as you begin to think about why and how you can use documents like this to justify what you are doing as you teach multimodal composing as described in this chapter. Thus, some highlights from each document:

- *21st-Century Literacies: A Policy Research Brief*: "Research shows that effective instruction in 21st-century literacies takes an integrated approach, helping students understand how to access, evaluate, synthesize, and contribute to information" (NCTE 2007, 5).
- ISTE NETS (National Educational Technology Standards): "[Students] interact, collaborate, and publish with peers, experts, or others employing a variety of digital environments and media" (2007, 1).
- 21st-Century Skills Map for English: "Acting on creative ideas to make a tangible and useful contribution to the domain in which the innovation occurs" (Partnership for 21st Century Skills with the National Council of Teachers of English 2008, 2).
- Michigan's high school content expectations for English language arts: "Compose written, spoken, and/or multimedia compositions in a range of genres (e.g., personal narrative, biography, poem, fiction, drama, creative nonfiction, summary, literary analysis essay, research report, or work-related text): pieces that serve a variety of purposes (e.g., expressive, informative, creative, and persuasive) and that use a variety of organizational patterns (e.g., autobiography, free verse, dialogue, comparison/contrast, definition, or cause and effect)" (Michigan Department of Education 2006, 6).

These are only examples of a broad range of expectations; and broad these expectations are, ranging from the technical aspects of using computers and the Internet to understanding how to write digitally for different audiences and purposes. Needless to say, we must consider the ways in which writers compose their work, and the MAPS heuristic helps us frame that discussion. It is with that in mind that I now turn to a discussion of how multimedia—image, audio, and video—can be used as tools for digital writing and, in turn, how we can teach students to examine author's craft in each of these media. Using multimedia, as has been demonstrated throughout this text and other contributions to our professional literature in recent years, including the standards documents noted earlier, is not just an add-on to our writing curriculum. As teachers of writing, and of digital writing, this is our content; more importantly, as multimedia continues to change, we need to accommodate those changes as we teach writing.

Thus, we will consider ways in which three different media for digital writing—photo-essays, podcasts, and digital stories—can be examined in light of conversations about author's craft. Like print, multimedia writing has certain elements of author's craft that can be explored in minilessons, replicated in students' writing, and evaluated on their effectiveness. Here, I do not offer step-by-step instructions for each of these types of digital writing tasks, as many online tutorials do this better than I can in the space of this book (again, return to the book's social network for links: digitalwritingworkshop.ning.com/). Instead, I examine the demands that each of these texts has for a writer, and I frame the discussion of each by offering a brief example and then look at the task of composing multimedia through MAPS.

Composing Digital Pictures and Creating Photo-Essays with Online Photo Sharing

To reiterate the cliché, a picture is worth a thousand words. And a picture with a smart caption, combined with just a few other photos, can be worth even more. That is the premise behind composing photo-essays. Composing photographs, and series of photographs, like writing, has the power to move people.

As both a means for inquiry and social action, Caroline Wang and Mary Ann Burris (1997) developed the idea of PhotoVoice. According to the PhotoVoice organization's website, its purpose is to "encourage the use of documentary photography by enabling those that have traditionally been the subject of such work to become its creator—to have control over how they are perceived by the rest of the world, while simultaneously learning a new skill which can enhance their lives" (www.photovoice.org/html/whoarewe/). Throughout the world, participants in PhotoVoice projects have used the power of images to compose their own stories, from their own perspectives. To see an example of how this works for students, I suggest viewing the work of Life Academy High School of Health and Bioscience teachers Clifford Lee and Brooke Fitzgerald, who worked with students to develop WHYS Up! A Critical Look at the San Francisco Bay Area, from the Perspectives of East Oakland

Youth, a blog that documented students' experience with community-based writing aimed at issues of social justice: whysupoakland.blogspot.com/. In much the same manner as described in the PhotoVoice methodology, Lee and Fitzgerald worked with their students to document social action projects throughout their community, highlighting the ways in which adolescents could make positive contributions to the area.

Digital cameras—and now, mobile phones with built-in cameras—allow us to capture and share images in ways unimagined just a few years ago. As more and more of us have gained access to smaller and increasingly inexpensive digital cameras, we have been able to simply take more and more pictures. Moreover, with the advent of online photo-sharing services such as Flickr (www.flickr.com/), Picasa (www.picasa.google.com/), Facebook (www.facebook.com/), and other tools, we are able to share our photos across time and space in a way that we have not been able to do before. These tools allow us to organize photos into collections and annotate our photos with hyperlinks or rollovers that display additional text or the names of people in the photos.

And that is where a powerful photo-essay can begin.

Note that students can create photo-essays using these services by creating albums and then captioning their pictures. Or, like Lee and Fitzgerald, they could create a blog. Or even a wiki. The possibilities for creating and organizing a photo-essay are limitless, yet these photo-sharing sites make organizing, tagging, and captioning photos much easier, and these services allow others to comment on the photos. Many teachers have also taken to using VoiceThread (voicethread.com/), a service that allows users to annotate photos by recording messages that are then attached to the designated pictures.

While I will not elaborate on the exact steps it takes to create an album through different photo-sharing services, as you can find instructions for those types of tasks on their respective websites, I will encourage you to think here about how individual photos—as well as entire photo-essays—are composed. That is, what does a digital writer do to think both as a photographer trying to frame a shot as well as someone who is composing a text, be it for arguing, entertaining, or informing? Thinking about the types of photos one needs to make a coherent photo-essay takes planning, and it can include both photos the digital writer takes as well as ones that are available online. The consideration here, of course, is that digital writers must be conscious of how they use the images of others, whether copyrighted or copyright friendly, as well as their own.

To elaborate: Like other forms of media, many photos found online are subject to copyright. And, clearly, students can find any number of photos online through a simple search. As mentioned in Chapter 1 and discussed in much greater detail in the Center for Social Media's *Code of Best Practices in Fair Use for Media Literacy Education* (2008; available at mediaeducationlab.com/sites/mediaeducationlab.com/files/CodeofBestPracticesinFairUse.pdf), provisions of the copyright law suggest that students can use any copyrighted images so long as the work that they create is transformative. This is important, because there are simply some pictures that a student might want to use in her essay that she could not take on her own such as, images of a foreign country to which the student has not traveled. So long as the student is employing the photo in a transformative manner and citing its source using a tool like Zotero, it would likely be considered fair use.

No matter what shape the photo-essay takes, however, I strongly encourage you to invite students to shoot their own photos rather than just find examples online, as that becomes a key part of the composing process. As students frame their images and, in turn, compose their entire essay, they can begin to explore the use of lighting, proximity, angles, and other photographic techniques to help highlight their subjects in different ways. (For more on the considerations involved in composing a photo-essay, see Figure 4.2.)

In sum, digital photo-essays offer students a chance to compose with both images and words, thus encouraging them to economize on words and think carefully about how they want individual images, as well as the order of images as a whole text, to work to create a mood and make a point. There are many examples online, and a web search for **Flickr photo-essay** will yield a number of results, and you can also start by visiting the Flickr group called Tell a Story in 5 Frames (www.flickr.com/groups/visualstory). As the title of the group implies, composers use only five images to tell an entire story, and this could work as an exercise for helping digital writers become more clear and concise. Whatever shape students' photo-essays take, using the commenting features offered by photo-sharing sites can be an ideal way to provide peer response to the photo-essays, much in the way that the commenting features of blogs allow for response, as discussed in Chapter 3.

Blending Voice, Music, and Sounds with Podcasts

Moving from the visual to the aural dimensions of digital writing, we can invite students to compose podcasts. Generally saved as an MP3 or other easily accessible audio file, a podcast is distributed online via an RSS feed. Many programs

FIGURE 4.2

MAPS for photo-essay

Mode	*Digital photo-essay*: Photo-essays are composed of any number of photographs that focus on a central theme. Typically, they are at least captioned, and they often have an introduction or conclusion that offers context to the images in the essay.
Media	*Digital photos*: Images can be scanned from original photos or artwork, and, of course, original images can be taken with a digital camera or cell phone. More importantly, where the images are hosted and shared determines what a digital writer can do with the images. Utilizing a service such as Flickr or Picasa allows the student to easily organize images into a collection and let others add comments. Also, a tool such as VoiceThread can allow the author to record his voice as an audio caption for each photo.
Audience	As with all digital writing, audiences will vary based on the overall goals of the assignment. Yet audiences viewing photo-essays will, in particular, be interested in the visual appeal of the subjects in relation to themselves. Digital writers should consider how they frame shots of human and nonhuman subjects to evoke emotions and convey a particular mood. Whether shots are staged or natural may become apparent to audiences as well.
Purpose	Purposes for photo-essays can vary widely. In the PhotoVoice project, cameras were given to everyday people in order to expose the poverty, corruption, and injustices around them. Students may simply create a photo-essay to document an event at school or in the community, or they may take an angle that leads toward a larger theme, such as courage or community.
Situation for the Writer and of the Writing Context	Digital writers who compose photo-essays will need to consider a variety of factors as they prepare to create their work. Some questions include • Do I have access to a digital camera, and if not, how can I get one? What additional equipment will I need? • Given the subject of my photo-essay, will I be able to take all the photos that I need on my own, or will I have to rely on other photographers to take images? Moreover, will I have to use stock photo galleries of copyright-free images or Creative Commons images? What images can I use under provisions of fair use? • If I am taking pictures of people specifically for my essay, what kinds of photo releases will I need? • Will my essay be organized chronologically or thematically? (in regard to composing the individual photos and the entire photo-essay) • How can I employ use of color, lighting, angles, zoom, and other effects to enhance the subjects of the photos?

such as iTunes can syndicate your podcast subscriptions by automatically downloading new episodes and transferring them to your MP3 player. Of course, you can also just listen to a podcast straight from the website at which it is posted, or if in a blog, via an RSS reader such as Google Reader. For a more technical description of this recording process, visit the book's companion website for links (digitalwritingworkshop.ning.com/) and view Chris Sloan's Audacity tutorials (www.judgememorial.com/sloan/audacity/).

Podcasts create an audio composing space that offers writers unique opportunities for expression. Robert Rozema describes the process of composing a "book talk"–style podcast and the effect that it should have on its audience:

> Finally, as in the case of all online publishing, podcasting about books gives students a real audience. My university students write their podcasts for an adolescent audience, creating short and appealing podcasts after the movie trailer model. Like movie trailers, their podcasts must begin with an engaging hook, reveal details about the plot but not say too much, and move toward a dramatic conclusion that leaves the audience wanting more. The students know that a podcast without an interesting opener will quickly lose its audience; a podcast without well-chosen excerpts and multiple voices will bore its audience; and a podcast without brisk pacing and an overall emotional impression will leave its audience flat. They write with adolescents in mind—young readers with short attention spans. (2008, 67)

Rozema also outlines the process his students went through to compose a particular mode of podcasts, an alternative to traditional book reports. By combining dialogue from characters in the book with dramatic music and appropriate sound effects, students created podcasts to sell their books to other readers, much the way movie trailers do.

This is one particular mode for podcasts. Another that educators are using is based on a series of personal essays from National Public Radio's This I Believe series (www.thisibelieve.org/). In their essay, writers focus on a key belief and develop their essay around that belief, citing personal stories that have strengthened their convictions. Dawn Reed, a high school teacher in Okemos, Michigan, and teacher consultant with the Red Cedar Writing Project, has used a This I Believe assignment to engage writers in the aural composing process, noting their increased sense of engagement and willingness to revise and rerecord their essays throughout the project (Reed and Hicks 2009). You can see how she structures her curriculum in Figure 4.3 and listen to her students' podcasts at reedd504.edublogs.org/.

FIGURE 4.3

Dawn Reed's curriculum for the This I Believe podcasting project

by Dawn Reed

The following steps are roughly the sequence that my class took to create podcasts. These steps took place over the course of a four-week unit in which I taught for a ninety-minute block schedule each day.

Days 1 and 2

1. Students read and discuss Grossman's article from *Time* magazine "The Time Person of the Year in 2006 is You."
2. Students write a brief reaction to the reading, answering these questions: What questions do you have about technology in our world? What is interesting to you? What points might you agree or disagree with in the article?
3. Further discuss the *Time* article and previous experiences with technology.
4. Silent discussion: Post questions around the room and have students respond on sticky notes (yellow for original posts, blue for responses to other questions). Use this silent discussion to lead into a conversation about the way blogs work and to further the conversation about technology use in our world and our class.

Discussion Questions

- How could larger audiences help you practice your speaking skills? Does the size of your audience influence your speech? How might the makeup (age, gender, location) of your audience influence your speech?
- How is peer response relevant to your development as a speaker? Would it be helpful to obtain feedback on your speaking skills from people outside of our classroom?
- How do you think technology will influence the way that speeches are given in the future? What sort of speeches do you expect to be giving in your future education? In your future career? What factors will be important to these speeches?
- The manner in which people voice their opinions and ideas is rapidly changing. In fact, many businesses are providing interactive technologies for their consumers. Even news reporters interact with their audience on blogs. While face-to-face speeches are still happening today, digital conferencing, meeting notes, and so on are incorporating technology. With this context in mind, how does technology influence what is expected of people today? How do these technologies influence speaking and communicating skills today?

FIGURE 4.3

Dawn Reed's curriculum for the This I Believe podcasting project (continued)

5. Wrap up discussion on the influence of technology on speeches in our world today. Students write a final reflection on the topic and make their first blog post.

   ### Reflection on the Influence of Technology on Speeches

   What points stood out to you from our discussion about the impact of technology on speeches? What aspects of technology in our world today are of interest to you? What other thoughts, specific issues, questions, or concerns would you like to address at this time, if any?

Days 3 and 4

6. As a class, listen to our first podcast from This I Believe (NPR 2007). Listen to Tony Hawk's (2007) essay "Do What You Love" (www.thisibelieve.org/dsp_ShowEssay.php?uid=22870) and discuss the essay.
7. Provide students with copies of the This I Believe curriculum and invite them to write a statement of beliefs. Students will begin to brainstorm ideas and share potential topics with others.

Days 5 and 6 (Class Held in Computer Lab)

8. To further generate ideas and get a sense of what the This I Believe essays are all about, students listen to several This I Believe podcasts and write a response to them.

   ### Listening Response

   Write a reaction to listening to the This I Believe essays. Consider a larger audience for your response. Let's have an online discussion and post these to our blog next week.

   - What do you understand about podcasting now?
   - Which This I Believe essays did you listen to? Why did you select those pieces? What aspects of the essays were memorable?

9. Students then visit Digital Voices (reedd504.edublogs.org/) or other sites where student podcasts have been posted and comment on at least one speech. Remember, students should use their first name only as a responder (follow school guidelines on student information being posted online). Often comments will not post right away; rather, a moderator will review the responses and then approve the comments.

(continues)

FIGURE 4.3

Dawn Reed's curriculum for the This I Believe podcasting project (continued)

Student Podcasting Examples

- Digital Voices (reedd504.edublogs.org/): This I Believe podcasts
- Beyond the Walls (english9reed.edublogs.org/): English 9 student work
- Basic English (shermansclass.edublogs.org/): This I Believe podcast
- Youth Voices Coast to Coast: NYC and Utah (youthvoices.net/): social networking with blogs and podcasts, too
- Jefferson Middle School Drama Program podcast (jefferson.podbean.com/)

10. As a class, discuss what is important for good comments on blog posts.

Days 7–14 (Using Computer Lab When Available)

11. Students continue to brainstorm and draft their This I Believe essay.
12. Students work with writing groups on the essay for peer review.
13. Plan introductions and closings of the speeches. Students generally write an introduction and a conclusion for their piece and invite a member of their writing group to record that portion of their speech.
14. As a class, discuss a class introductory clip. Develop a class plan for the introduction. Record beliefs and learn how to work in Audacity.

Days 15–20 (Using Computer Lab When Available)

15. Learn Audacity with Chris Sloan's (n.d.) screencasts, found at www.judgememorial.com/sloan/audacity/.
16. As students are continually revising and editing their essay, we also discuss the following: How does this type of speech require a clear speaking voice?
17. Workshop class: Students write, revise, edit, listen to podcasts, learn Audacity, and practice reading, and then they record the speech. Students also prepare their introduction and conclusion and ask a classmate to record their introduction and conclusion. Students then edit the speech and piece the sections together.
18. When students are working on finalizing their podcast, as a class we discuss publicizing our work. Together we create fliers for the school hallways, send emails to potential audience members, and invite other classes to listen in.
19. Students publish their work to the class blog.
20. Students listen to one another's podcasts and comment on their peer's blog posts.
21. Students create a reflection on the podcasting project.

FIGURE 4.3

Dawn Reed's curriculum for the This I Believe podcasting project (continued)

INFORMATIVE SPEECH: THIS I BELIEVE ASSIGNMENT

Objectives

- Develop an informative speech drawing from your own knowledge of life through an informative statement of personal belief.
- Select a worthwhile subject for your This I Believe essay, naming a specific belief. It should follow the This I Believe guidelines of being about a personal belief. Name a belief and show the importance of that belief through story or personal examples that you deem acceptable to share. The subject of your speech should be relevant, important, and of value to your audience.
- Present your speech through the recording of your essay.
- Engage in a speech genre popular to our society through development and delivery of your own This I Believe essay based on the National Public Radio invitation.
- Gain confidence with your potential as a speaker.
- Obtain a wider audience through the possibility of posting your speech online in an MP3 format for our speech class podcast.
- Collaborate with classmates to develop an introduction to your speech to be given by a classmate. Learn how to develop an introduction for another speaker.

Length

- 350- to 500-word essay
- total length with introduction and additional editing: four to eight minutes maximum

Requirements

1. This I Believe essay (350 to 500 words), in typed format and recorded in audio as an MP3
2. essay follows This I Believe guidelines: focuses on a belief, represents a personal statement of belief, maintains positive tone, gives clear examples to support the belief
3. clear, specific, detailed information that proves the relevance of the belief to the speaker
4. logical progressions and clear transitions
5. appropriate and relevant topic
6. adequate preparation and information—speech should show time and effort
7. developed essay and introduction of a classmate's essay are part of this speech project
8. in-class participation: responding to other speeches

(continues)

FIGURE 4.3

Dawn Reed's curriculum for the This I Believe podcasting project (continued)

Name: _____

INFORMATIVE SPEECH EVALUATION

This I Believe Essay

Content (40)

_____/10   This I Believe essay (350 to 500 words), in typed format and recorded in audio as an MP3.

_____/10   Essay follows This I Believe guidelines: focuses on a belief, represents a personal statement of belief, maintains a positive tone, gives clear examples to support the belief. The essay provides a clear overall point or message.

_____/10   Clear, specific, detailed information that proves the relevance of the belief to the speaker is present in the essay and conveyed through the speaking voice of the presenter. The essay and performance have logical progressions and clear transitions.

_____/10   Developed essay shows speaker's unique style and voice. Essay is edited (grammar, usage, and mechanics do not disrupt readability).

Delivery (10)

_____/10   The speaker's voice shows interest and appropriate emotion to complement speech. Rate, volume, and variety complement the speech.

Content and Voice Delivery (10)

_____/ 5   Developed introduction complements the speaker.

_____/ 5   Voice shows interest to complement the speaker.

Response to Other Speeches

_____/10   Thoughtful and specific response to other speeches shared with speakers through blog comments.

Final Reflection on Podcasting Project

_____/15   Typed reflection explains what the speaker learned from sharing his or her work with a larger audience, developing a speech focusing solely on voice, being a part of a larger project through NPR's This I Believe project, and recording, editing, and podcasting a speech.

_____/90   Total

FIGURE 4.3

Dawn Reed's curriculum for the This I Believe podcasting project (continued)

THIS I BELIEVE INFORMATIVE SPEECH AND PODCASTING REFLECTION

Compose a one-page-minimum typed reflection explaining what you learned from the This I Believe podcasting project. Be sure to consider the following: the assignment of writing a This I Believe essay, inspired by National Public Radio's This I Believe series, to take part in a larger speaking invitation; recording and editing in Audacity; the process of recording and editing your voice; the role of pace and variety in speaking; developing a speech focusing solely on voice; sharing your speech with a larger audience; and hearing your own voice on the World Wide Web. Be specific in your response by using concrete examples about the process and the product of your work. Also consider how you would rate your own work according to the informative speech rubric for this project. You may also address what you have learned about the role of technology in communication and speeches in our world today.

References

Audacity: Free Audio Editor and Recorder. Retrieved November 12, 2008, from audacity.source forge.net/.

Grossman, Lev. 2006. "Time's Person of the Year: You." *Time* December 25: 40–41.

Hawk, Tony. 2007. "Do What You Love." Retrieved April 23, 2007, from www.npr.org/templates/ story/story.php?storyId=5568583.

National Public Radio. 2007. This I Believe. Website. Retrieved April 3, 2007, from www.npr.org/ templates/story/story.php?storyId=4538138.

Sloan, Chris. n.d. Audacity Tutorials. Retrieved November 12, 2008, from www.judgememorial .com/sloan/audacity/.

As you can see, podcasts can take a variety of modes from a personal essay to a book response, and they can range from a simple recording of one writer reading his work to entire class productions, such as the *Room 208* podcast, much like a newscast, produced by Bob Sprankle's students (www.bobsprankle .com/blog/). In terms of media, again, podcasts certainly involve students sharing their voices, literally, through speaking, singing, and dramatic acting as well as the additional options of including music and sound effects. As a multimedia composing process, podcasting allows writers to use the power of tone and inflection, blending tracks and adjusting volume to create just the right effect. By inviting students to use their voice to bring life to a piece of writing, we can help them understand the ways in which oral and written language differ, thus broadening their repertoire of both writing and speaking strategies. Figure 4.4 outlines the MAPS for podcasting and explores these ideas in more depth.

FIGURE 4.4

MAPS for podcasting	
Mode	As noted previously, podcasts can take a variety of modes, including a personal essay, a book response, a newscast, an interview, a variety show, or any other kind of recording. This occurs with one person reading her writing or a series of writers enacting a drama or creating a show. The National Public Radio program "This American Life" also offers a unique genre that blends human interest topics with compelling storytelling.
Media	Because podcasts are ultimately shared as audio files, often as MP3s, digital writers have to have access to an audio editor, such as the free and open-source program Audacity (audacity.sourceforge.net/). Podcasts need to be hosted somewhere, either as an upload on a blog or wiki site or on a school or personal web server. Some podcasting services exist as well, yet storage capacity for those services varies, so be sure to identify a space that will be able to handle your needs.
Audience	Most likely, the audience members for a podcast will be listening at their computer or through an MP3 player. Thus, as Rozema (2008) argues, the podcast should be compelling and offer the listener a reason to continue listening within the opening moments. Reed, for instance, worked with her students to develop an audio intro modeled after the original This I Believe series so that listeners could identify each podcast in the series and know exactly when information about the author and essay would be presented.
Purpose	Based on the choice of mode, the purpose for podcasts can vary widely from simply sharing an interview to producing a more complex composition such as a newscast, book talk, or other academic style of talk. No matter what the purpose, composers should be aware of the format and be sure to offer introductory information in the podcast that will somehow make the purpose clear to the listener.
Situation for the Writer and of the Writing Context	The writer will need to practice his speaking voice, perhaps adjusting the written text to better match the patterns of the spoken word. In order to compose podcasts, writers will need to have access to digital voice recorders, a microphone and headset, and a computer with an audio editor installed. Since audio files can begin to grow large quickly, they will have to have access to adequate network space for saving their projects or access to a podcasting service such as odeo.com or podomatic.com. Additional music from services like freeplaymusic.com and sound effects from services like freesound.org can enhance the overall effect of the podcast. Finally, they will have to be able to convert their projects into an audio format readable by all media players, such as MP3 or WAV, and to post that file on a publicly accessible website or blog.

When students compose podcasts—mixing their own voice with additional sound effects, music, and, perhaps, the voices of others—they learn how to make a textured composition, one in which many subtle aspects of the work that could simply be considered as background noise actually magnify the work in ways that just an author reading her piece could not achieve on her own. Thus, it stands to reason that bringing the aural elements that podcasting allows together with the visual ones that a photo-essay allow can lead to an entirely different form of multimedia writing: a digital video.

Combining Voice, Video, Image, and Text Through Digital Video Production

Digital video production, like podcasting, is simple to define in technical terms yet defies simple description as a particular mode of writing. In terms of the technical aspects, digital video production merges a combination of any or all of the following into a concise fiction or nonfiction video: text, spoken voice, still and moving images, music, sound effects, and transitions or other video effects. In particular, the term *digital storytelling* has been coined to describe the ways in which digital writers compose fiction and creative nonfiction texts through the production of digital videos. To return to the Educause series "7 Things You Should Know About...," the authors define digital storytelling as "the practice of combining narrative with digital content, including images, sound, and video, to create a short movie, typically with a strong emotional component" (net.educause.edu/ir/library/pdf/ELI7021.pdf).

Certainly, there are other modes that writers using the medium of digital video can produce, as noted with the example of PSAs in the beginning of this chapter. To that end, and to reiterate the distinction between mode and medium, I find it important to help students understand that a digital story is one mode in which they can compose with the medium of digital video production, and another is a PSA. Making these differentiations is important for us as writing teachers; otherwise, students will think everything being created as a movie is a digital story and will not define the task of creating their videos more clearly in terms of mode, audience, and purpose. For the sake of this example, I elaborate more on the mode of digital storytelling and encourage you to think about these ideas in relation to other modes that could be created, such as PSAs, commercials, newscasts, satire, or, to expand on Rozema's idea, video-based book talk–style trailers.

In terms of digital storytelling, then, and getting to the point about having an emotional component, Bernajean Porter (2009), author of *DigiTales: The Art of Telling Digital Stories* (2005), describes the ways in which authors can use multimedia effects to accentuate their work. At a basic level, a digital writer can use an effect to "decorate" his digital story. In this manner, a particular piece of media (such as clip art) or effect (such as a transition) would be used to simply fill space or to fulfill a requirement of the assignment (such as that a writer includes a certain number of pictures). In short, it adds little to the digital story or, worse yet, detracts from the story's overall effectiveness.

Porter then suggests that media or effects can be used to "illustrate" a digital story; in that case, the item adds value to the story that could not have been expressed only through written text. For instance, instead of spending twenty seconds of a digital story to describe a person, a digital writer may insert an image of that person and focus only on one key characteristic in the spoken narrative. This both saves time in the overall narrative—important, as digital stories are generally about three to five minutes long—and allows the writer the opportunity to use her words to make points that the pictures may not be able to make, such as discussing actions that further describe the character.

At another level, Porter argues that a particular piece of media or an effect can be used to "illuminate" a point. For instance, in the digital story "Meet Vinnie," created by my Chippewa River Writing Project colleague, Shannon Powell, she describes the first year of her son's life throughout the story, discussing the many roles that he has played over the course of the year, such as "sleeper," "karaoke mascot," "entertainer," and "Mommy's outdoor helper" (www.youtube.com/watch?v=ZW-cZ5qdTyQ). With the audience of her family in mind, she uses her narration to build up to the climax of the story, pointing out that Vinnie will soon have a new role. Then, instead of narrating, she presents the conclusion of the story as a final slide with an announcement of just a few words, which you will have to view for yourself to understand the full effect of how it "illuminates" the story.

By illustrating or illuminating the text in an appropriate manner, the digital writer employs multimedia for a maximum effect. These rhetorical considerations are critical for digital writers as they engage in the writing process. For instance, when describing the process of composing digital stories, Sara Kajder (2004) argues that her students did not focus solely on the technologies, a complaint that she feared from other colleagues. Instead, their thinking changed.

New understanding shaped and drove a revision of former ideas and practices. Content and writing drove this assignment. The technology was simply a delivery tool that ultimately provided a hook that tapped into students' existing visual and technological literacies. (65)

The new understanding, then, is what becomes critical in this process of multimodal authoring. For instance, to return to the image in Chapter 1 and the reflections of a teacher engaged in the process of teaching students to compose digital video, Aram Kabodian (2008) asks a number of questions that you must consider when beginning the process of composing digital stories:

- "How do I incorporate digital storytelling into my curriculum in a way that meets students where they're at, complements their knowledge, thoughts, and feelings, and challenges each student in meaningful ways …and still ensure that I teach my entire curriculum?
- "Should a digital story begin with an idea/assignment or with photos?"
- "How can I possibly get enough computers often enough to create digital stories?
- "How many digital stories do I need to create before I feel competent enough to lead my students in the process?
- "Is teaching the writing part of a digital story different than teaching writing as I usually teach it? And if so, how?"

In asking these questions, Kabodian articulates both the logistical concerns (getting computers) as well as the personal (Am I confident enough to do this?) and pedagogical concerns that you might encounter in the process of creating digital stories. These question lead into the MAPS for composing digital videos, as outlined in Figure 4.5.

In terms of structuring multimedia writing assignments, especially those involving digital video, teachers need to consider a number of concerns with both the content and the form, especially if students are creating a nonfiction text that is meant to persuade. For instance, Sharon Murchie, a teacher at Bath High School and teacher consultant for the Red Cedar Writing Project, invites her seniors to create PSAs as a component of their senior project (projectwritemsu .wikispaces.com/Murchie_lessons). As Figure 4.6 demonstrates, she does describe particular requirements in both content and form of the PSA, consequently guiding her students as conscientious researchers throughout the early stages of their projects so that they can make cogent arguments in their PSAs as well as cite their sources.

FIGURE 4.5

MAPS for digital video

Mode
Mode sometimes becomes a point of contention when creating digital video. Porter (2009) worries that many digital video productions are being called digital stories, yet they may be nonfiction texts and lack a narrative structure with a compelling theme. Thus, I encourage you to be intentional in discussing the mode of digital video production with your students. Compare, for instance, the characteristics of fiction or memoir when composing digital stories with the more persuasive characteristics of creating a public service announcement or informational characteristics of creating a documentary.

Media
Creating digital stories is both a bit more complex than composing a podcast and more platform dependent; that is, one must know the video editing software and be able to work within it with media as well as export files to an easily readable format. On Macs, the prepackaged program is iMovie, and on PCs it is Windows Movie Maker. Also, PC users can download the free Photo Story 3 program.

Files exported from these programs are generally readable with any media player, although a viewer may need to install extra features (for instance, QuickTime on the Mac requires an extension to play native Windows movies, WMV files). One way to avoid this problem, as well as the additional problem of transferring media with something such as a flash drive, is to use a web-based video editing service such as MovieMasher (www.moviemasher.com/)

Audience
Like photo-essays and podcasts, digital videos of all modes will aim to capture the audience's attention and have a consistent theme throughout so that the audience remains engaged. Care should be taken to use narration, audio, images, and video to create a story that, as Porter (2009) argues, is illuminating for the audience, not simply a collection of video effects.

Purpose
As with other new media, the purposes for digital video production can vary widely. Broadly, it is important to consider whether the purpose will be to create a narrative or poetic video as compared with an informational or persuasive one. Thus, defining a clear purpose for the project before production even begins is crucial, as Sharon Murchie did in her Senior Seminar Final Project, shown in Figure 4.6.

Situation for the Writer and of the Writing Context
Writers will have to be at least basically familiar with the process of creating a movie—importing media, organizing a time line, layering in transitions and other effects, adding voice-overs, and exporting the final file. Beyond these basics, writers will also have to be especially mindful of copyright when creating digital stories, as well as documenting their sources for images, videos, music, and files. Also, if digital writers are taking personal photographs or videos and using sound them in their stories, they will need to be sure to get permission from their subjects.

(continues)

FIGURE 4.5

MAPS for digital video (continued)

Creating digital video is a recursive process, one that requires digital writers to move from the video editing program to searching for images and sounds online and then back to their original narrative or script and revising it as the time line gets adjusted. Moreover, these compositions can take a great deal of time, thus requiring use of a computer lab or laptop cart for a number of days, ideally all in a row. Students' hard drive and/or network storage at school will need to accommodate a large number of audio, image, and video files. Finally, the piece needs to be saved and stored in an accessible format, ideally through a video sharing service such as YouTube (www.youtube.com), TeacherTube (www.teachertube.com), or Viddler (www.viddler.com), depending on the school's filtering policy.

In sum, creating digital videos—like creating photo-essays and podcasts—requires that writers begin the process with a clear sense of mode and purpose, as well as an understanding of what they need to learn about particular technologies in order to build their final projects. In nearly every instance that I have created or helped students and teachers create digital stories, I have found the same results that Kajder did when she worked with her students: creating a digital video can be a transformative experience for a writer. By continuing to focus on MAPS, and examine the craft that authors use to compose these types of texts, we can help our students learn how to create these powerful forms of digital writing.

Looking Ahead: Capturing Thinking with Screencasts

Examining author's craft in multimedia writing provides us with opportunities to engage in simultaneous discussions about words, images, sounds, and video, thus supporting the types of critical media literacies that students need to develop. As the ease of use for digital video continues to improve, and access to cameras (including those built in to laptops) becomes more ubiquitous, producing digital videos—in addition to photo-essays and podcasts—will become more and more a natural part of a digital writer's composing process.

FIGURE 4.6

Sharon Murchie's senior seminar final project assignment sheet

SENIOR SEMINAR FINAL PROJECT

Your final project should be a study of a topic that impacts you. Similar to "Did You Know: Shift Happens," your project should analyze your topic and have statistics, visuals, and a music file. (youtube.com/watch?v=pMcfrLYDm2U)

Requirements

- Work in a group of two or three. No exceptions. Groups must be established and reported by May 9.
- Your presentation topic should be something that impacts you, your generation, your future, and so on. Your presentation topic must be established and reported by May 12.
- Your presentation will be due on May 19 or 20. Your group must sign up for your presentation time and day by May 15.
- Your presentation should be from three to five minutes long. (No shorter than three minutes; no longer than five minutes.) If your presentation is too short or too long, your grade will be docked by the percentage of time it did not meet requirements.
- Your presentation must be school appropriate at all times.
- All statistics you state must be cited, both on the slide and in correct works cited format at the end.
- It is recommended that you use PowerPoint and a CD of your music file. This is the easiest way, using school software and equipment, to create your presentation. Save your PowerPoint in your H-drive; put the CD in the CD drive. (Use the tutorial link on I-cal to learn how to link your music track to your PowerPoint.) If you choose to use other software and other formats, it is your responsibility to ensure that it will play on the laptop in the mediated lecture hall.
- Your presentation is due on the day you sign up to present. It is your responsibility to ensure that your presentation is saved in an appropriate manner and will play on the laptop in the mediated lecture hall.

Grading

30 points: interesting, clear, and concise information in presentation (Note: This presentation must think *globally* and *into the future* to earn 30 points.)

20 points: interesting and professional visual slide layout

20 points: song file that adds depth to content

10 points: all statistics cited on each slide

20 points: correct works cited on last slide

Total points possible: 100

Another increasingly popular and easy tool for multimedia production is screencasting, which as the name implies allows digital writers to record what is happening on their screens. In a sense, a digital writer can compose an informational text about how to do a particular task onscreen or, more creatively, can develop a fictional story in which what happens on the computer—such as an IM chat—becomes part of the story. They could also narrate a slide show, discuss the process of revision in their writing while tracking changes, or any other onscreen task that can be recorded and reflected upon. While I can only speculate here on the possibilities that screencasting can offer in terms of a digital writing tool, I do feel that it is worth your time to try it out if for no other reason than to create a simple how-to video that documents some digital writing process such as exporting a file or adding a transition in a movie, a mode in which more and more of us need to compose as we teach students technology skills.

You can begin with Jing (jingproject.com/), a free and user-friendly screencasting tool. Offered by TechSmith, the same company that produces the more robust Camtasia Studio, Jing allows you to record up to five minutes in a screencast and quickly post it to your own account on www.screencast.com/. Whether you use it to visually describe a process (such as posting to a page on your class wiki) or create a more involved narrative, getting only one take to make your screencast forces you, as a digital writer, to make decisions about key ideas and how to organize those ideas so they are most effective for your viewers. Screencasting can make for a simple and effective way for teachers to demonstrate digital writing processes and for students to offer tours of their individual multimedia texts or entire portfolios.

No matter how screencasting or any of the other tools described in this chapter are used, they can continue to push our thinking about what it means to examine author's craft in digital writing, especially multimedia writing. It is with this idea in mind that we now turn our attention to how students can share their digital writing through the design and publication of blog-based portfolios, wiki-based anthologies, and audio collections of their work.

5 Designing and Publishing Digital Writing

For years, advocates of the writing workshop approach have been encouraging their students to share writing beyond the walls of the classroom. Many methods for sharing have been introduced into our classrooms, such as pen pal exchanges, whole-class read-arounds, celebrations of students' work using an author's chair, and published classwide or schoolwide anthologies. Moreover, with the advent of the Internet, many classes have begun creating class or school websites that showcase students' work. While the in-class readings of work take up time, they contribute to the feeling of community in many writing workshops. Unfortunately, creating these different collections of student work can be a time-consuming task for a single teacher, and it often takes away from the more important work of responding to writers while they are still in the writing process. Thus employing the tools described in this book for the purpose of publishing student work—and inviting outside audiences to comment on that work—may be the biggest advantage of composing with digital texts, allowing students a purposeful opportunity to share their voices with the world.

And, though all of these methods help students distribute their writing to wider audiences, the digital writing tools that are highlighted in this book bring a new sense of immediacy to the task. While the strategies outlined in the previous paragraph were highly teacher dependent in their nature—requiring educators to spend hours organizing a class anthology, for instance—students now have the ability to publish their work directly to the read/write web. Teachers can still monitor and edit what students post, of course, but as I've shown throughout this book, students now have the ability to post and share their work independently and instantaneously.

As students explore writing with newer technologies, their ability to share these texts with a wider audience exponentially increases. Class blogs, wikis, and podcasts offer students a chance to share work in progress or in final form. Digital portfolios can organize and display work across a school year or a school career. While some of the work that is published in this sense may not be of the quality that we would have considered publishable in the past—for instance, a brief blog post that was created in just a few minutes does not usually share the same qualities as a story crafted over many weeks—publishing digital writing also offers students the opportunity to share their ideas in progress. To reconsider our approach to teaching with digital writing, we need to move from a vision of publication as all final product to one in which students can post, revise, and repost over time.

While these opportunities are exciting, I recognize that digital spaces for publishing raise concerns for students, parents, teachers, and administrators about safety and risk. For students, it may simply be a question of social awkwardness: Will my readers like my writing? For parents, teachers, and administrators, there are a host of legal and ethical concerns that are too numerous to list here including issues related to privacy and copyright. Yet, for teachers, publishing digital writing has the potential to create a much different dynamic in the classroom. Typically, we are used to one-to-one, small-group, or whole-class instruction in writing. With digital writing, the audience is extended, and students become much more aware, as readers and as writers, of how they both share their work and respond to the work of others.

The process of students publishing their writing in terms of design and distribution contributes to the success of individual writers and the overall writing workshop community. In terms of design, students can create personal digital portfolios, class anthologies with wikis, and audio anthologies of their work. In terms of distribution, the types of digital writing that students can design for all three of these technologies are somewhat interchangeable; for instance, it is easy for students to record audio and post it to their own blog in the form of a podcast or share it via a class multimedia anthology. That said, I focus here on one particular technology for each digital writing application and offer some advice about how to extend the possibilities with each.

Before moving forward, it should be noted that there are a number of places where students can publish their work online beyond our classrooms, some of it through informal posting to a website and some of it through more formal processes that undergo review by communities of readers and writers. Colin

Lankshear and Michele Knobel (2006) discuss a number of ways in which writers are able to share their work, most notably through fan fiction.

> Fan fictions chronicle alternative adventures, mishaps, or even invented histories or futures for main characters; relocate main characters from a series or movie to a new universe altogether; create "prequels" for shows or movies; fill in plot holes; or realize relationships between characters that were only hinted at, if that, within the original text. (86)

Lankshear and Knobel elaborate on the many ways that writers collaborate to publish their work, mainly through the act of coauthoring pieces and offering substantial peer review to others' work. One such community is located at www.fanfiction.net/. There are many other places where writers can go to share their work, such as e-zines (electronic magazines that have no hard copy counterparts).

While these types of sites are important and useful for adolescent writers—and many students engage in writing for these types of sites during their out-of-school time—there are other ways that students can harness digital writing tools to create their own personal portfolios, class anthologies, and, ideally, develop communities across classrooms. In other words, I want to encourage you as a digital writing teacher to help your students understand how to create and manage their own spaces for digital writing. It is important for them to learn how to contribute to their own communities of digital writers, all while learning how to create their own portfolios or participate in a wiki around a shared sense of topic and purpose.

Publication and Response

Writers write to be read. Many of the teacher researchers mentioned earlier in this text, especially Nancie Atwell (1998), remind us of this fact. Response becomes an important part of the publication rituals that we engage our students in as readers and writers.

Like all innovations, digital writing presents opportunities and challenges for our students and for us as teachers. On the one hand, when students are responsible for posting their own writing and commenting on the writing of others, they are likely to feel more engaged in the writing process. By reading what others have written, they gather both ideas for their own writing as well as different elements of author's craft that can help make their writing better. The process of commenting on others' work can help writers identify what works, and what does not work, when thinking about creating their own pieces. Yet students can also become distracted by publishing their own work and may not engage fully in the process of peer response. They may get caught up in stylistic elements such as changing fonts or adding hyperlinks without thinking rhetorically about what such moves add to their piece of writing. Their comments can be superficial, and not help their peers or themselves grow as writers.

To address concerns such as these in the peer response process, the National Writing Project's (2008) online writing community, E-Anthology, has developed a simple model for peer response that invites the writer to ask for the specific kind of response that he is seeking. Writers who post to the E-Anthology are asked to tell readers whether they want their work to be "blessed," "addressed," or "pressed." If you are new to the online community, or feel that your piece is very personal and do not want it to be critiqued heavily, you might ask for a responder to bless it by simply offering praise. Inviting readers to address the piece means that you have specific questions about it, such as about character development or the flow, and want feedback on that. Finally, if you want a reader to press in his response, you are willing to accept any critiques that could help you move toward a stronger version of your writing. For all three methods of response, the author identifies what she is seeking and invites responders to give appropriate feedback, a method that works well any time a writer is seeking response, online or offline.

With this model for response in mind as one possible way for students to interact with one another as they move their work toward publication, we can employ three types of digital writing tools for individual and classroom publication. As noted earlier, there are safety and ethical concerns with publishing student work online, too, but they are surmountable. Moreover, standards and curriculum reforms as well as shifts in our thinking about writing pedagogy are pushing toward more authentic purposes and audiences as well as varied genres. Thus, the opportunity to publish digital writing is critical for students—both to learn the technical aspects of doing so as well as to reach wider audiences.

Digital Portfolios

Through the work of many teacher researchers and composition scholars, the idea of creating a writing portfolio has become an integral part of teaching in the writing workshop (see, for instance, the edited collections of Graves and

Sunstein [1992] and Yancey and Weiser [1997]). By collecting examples of their work over the course of time, and by reflecting on their revision process, students articulate what they believe they have learned about the writing process and about themselves as writers. Through a combination of self-assessment and teacher evaluation based on set criteria, writers gain insights into their strengths and weaknesses.

In the broadest sense, then, a digital portfolio is a similar collection of students' writing presented through a particular technology, often as a website or slide show. By structuring the portfolio with a table of contents that allows for easy navigation as well as other features such as a links to reflective statements or previous drafts, digital writers can take advantage of the media to present a more robust portrait of their work as writers. Moreover, they are able to present other kinds of digital writing beyond simply sharing text; integrating audio, video, and images into a digital portfolio has become easier and easier with the advent of read/write web technologies.

One particular technology that was outlined earlier in this book and will be employed in a slightly different manner now is blogs. While blogs are typically meant to serve in the sense of how I discussed them earlier—as an ongoing collection of posts that invite responses and build toward longer, more involved pieces—the blogs that you invite your digital writers to create can easily be transformed into a digital portfolio. Some people refer to this hybrid use as a *blogfolio*, and the numerous design options that blogs offer create a unique opportunity for a digital writer to make a personalized portfolio without having to design a web page from scratch.

Other options for creating digital portfolios exist, including designing and uploading web pages with a program such as Adobe's Dreamweaver, Microsoft's Expression, or Apple's iWeb, but these require that you have server space to upload your files. Also, a number of sites such as Google Sites (sites.google.com/), Yahoo!'s Geocities (geocities.yahoo.com/), and Webs (www.webs.com/) can be used, but generally they have advertising on them. For these reasons, my example uses WordPress, a free and open-source blogging platform that your school can install on its own server or that you can have students access through edublogs.org/ or wordpress.com.

How to Make Digital Portfolios with Blogs

Creating a blogfolio requires a few steps that will tweak the settings on your blog as well as create a page for your portfolio's home and navigation. Unlike the typical post that a digital writer creates for her blog, which eventually rolls off the home screen into the blog archives, a page becomes a permanent feature on the blog, typically getting its own hyperlink along the top navigation bar.

As noted previously, there are a number of tools you could use to create a digital portfolio, many outlined by Helen Barrett on her Electronic Portfolios homepage (electronicportfolios.org/). For sake of example, and as a way for you to think about how you might set up a portfolio using the other tools mentioned earlier, here are the steps for setting up a WordPress blog through Edublogs to become a digital portfolio. These instructions assume that you have already begun an account, as discussed in Chapter 3. Other blogging platforms and services such as the free Class Blogmeister (www.classblogmeister.com/) and Blogger (www.blogger.com/) or the fee-based TypePad (www.typepad.com/) differ slightly in terms of layout and function, so you will have to explore how to create a static page in those programs. Please note that while you are setting up your blog to have a distinct homepage and links to particular posts that are associated as portfolio pieces, the existing posts will not disappear. Instead, they will be archived on the blog. In this way, a blog actually serves as an excellent digital writing tool because, if the student has tagged individual posts well over time, it will essentially become an archive of his work, and the portfolio will be a showcase for that archive. To review the process of how to make posts, return to Chapter 3. To create a blogfolio by linking to existing posts within your blog, follow these directions:

1. Set up a portfolio page. Your portfolio, again, will be a page that is a permanent fixture on your blog, distinct from a regular post. Therefore, it is important to follow these directions in order for it to show up properly in your navigation bar and have a succinct URL.
   a. In the Edublogs administrative panel called the Dashboard, under the Write tab, select Page (see Figure 5.1).
   b. For the title, enter **Portfolio,** and for text in the page itself, enter the number of pieces you plan to include. In Figure 5.1, for example, I have listed four: Piece 1, Piece 2, Piece 3, and Piece 4.
   c. Save the page and then click on Visit Site. Depending on the theme you have chosen for your blog, because some do not display pages automatically, you should see a button in the navigation bar called Portfolio. Click on that link and you will see the results of your work so far.
   d. Return to the Dashboard by selecting Edit This on your page in the blog's public view. Typically, this will be a link at the bottom of the post.

FIGURE 5.1

Setting up a portfolio page in Edublogs

2. Set up links to pieces in the portfolio. For each piece that you want to link to in your portfolio, you will need to get the stable URL for the piece and create a hyperlink to it from your portfolio's main page. I find it easiest to do this by having one tab in my browser open to the Dashboard, where I am editing the portfolio page, and another tab opened to my blog, where I can click on individual posts. Remember that URLs on blogs can be tricky. Your blog has a main URL, such as mine at hickstro.org/. But individual posts have their own stable URL, too, often with a combination of the date and post title in it, such as hickstro.org/2009/02/07/notes-from-rcwp-google-day/. Remember, you don't want to link only to the homepage of the blog, because that post will eventually disappear from the homepage as more are added; thus, it is critical that you link to the post directly. Also, posts allow for comments and—as noted earlier—the author can seek responses from peers that bless, address, or press their work that can then be posted to the comment section for each piece.

a. Navigate to the post that you want to include as one of your links in the portfolio.

b. Highlight and then copy the URL for that post from the navigation bar.

c. Click back into the portfolio page you are editing. Highlight one of the placeholder titles (e.g., Piece 1) and type in the actual name of the piece you are linking to. (See Figure 5.2.)

d. Highlight the title of the piece and hit the Hyperlink button.

e. Paste the URL in the text box that appears. Also, set the target to Open Link in Same Window.

f. Repeat this process for as many links to different pieces as you have in your portfolio.

3. Set the portfolio page as the homepage for your blog. While this step may not be absolutely necessary, I find it easier to review students' work when they all set their blog to have the portfolio as their homepage, at least temporarily, while I am doing final evaluations. That way, when you link to their blog, you are automatically taken to their portfolio homepage and avoid any confusion in finding it.

a. Select the Settings tab, on the right, and then select Reading. (See Figure 5.3.)

b. Under Front Page Displays, choose A Static Page and then select the Portfolio page.

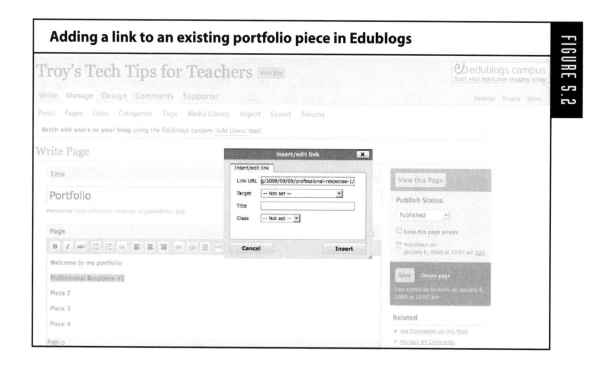

Adding a link to an existing portfolio piece in Edublogs

FIGURE 5.2

FIGURE 5.3

Creating a static homepage for your portfolio in Edublogs

Troy's Tech Tips for Teachers Visit Site

eb edublogs campus
Start your institution blogging today!

Write   Manage   Design   Comments   Supporter

Settings   Plugins   Users

General   Writing   Reading   Discussion   Privacy   Miscellaneous   Delete Blog   FeedBurner   Blog Type   Blog Avatar

Batch add users to your blog using the Edublogs custom 'Add Users' tool.

Reading Settings

Front page displays
- ○ Your latest posts
- ● A static page (select below)
  - • Front page: Portfolio
  - • Posts page: – Select –

Blog pages show at most   10   posts

Syndication feeds show the most recent   10   posts

For each article in a feed, show
- ● Full text
- ○ Summary

c. Scroll down to select Save Changes and then visit the site to make sure that the portfolio page comes up as the homepage.

In sum, the benefits of creating digital portfolios have been widely discussed by writing teachers and scholars for a number of years. Creating a digital portfolio "asks students to write *for the screen* as well as *for the page*; to create relationships between and among linked material, as between and among experiences; to update it as a habit of mind; and to represent learning in part by exploring the connections the digital environment invites" (Yancey 2004, 754). By using a blog as the medium to house their portfolio, students are able to customize the design of their portfolio through the way that they set up the homepage as well as the theme that they choose. Instead of worrying about extensive HTML coding, other technical aspects of creating a web page, or the many functions of expansive software packages, they are able to focus more on the content that they want to present. Thus, they are able to, as Yancey notes, "represent learning" in ways that allow for individual expression while still demonstrating deep understanding of their writing and revising process.

Class Anthologies

For years, writing teachers have helped students share their stories through classroom anthologies of their writing. Typically, each student contributes a short piece and an editor, or editing team, compiles all the pieces into a single document, the anthology. These anthologies can be very simple, created by just copying and pasting pieces into a word processor, or they can be much more thoroughly designed with desktop publishing software. No matter how they are designed, anthologies are generally printed and bound in some fashion, with copies distributed to the students at the end of the project.

As I have noted in the other sections of this chapter, this type of publication ritual was—and still is—important. Students want to see their name in print. Yet the conventions and cost of print limit how many copies we can make and how far we can distribute them. Moreover, as anthologies accumulate on the shelves of our classroom libraries, it takes a conscious effort to pull them out so current students can see what was written before. As many teachers are, I am pressed for time, and I know that years of my anthologies, sadly, never saw the light of day again after the end of the school year.

Thus, creating a class anthology with a wiki offers a few advantages that could, potentially, engage students in the process and help them organize their work, search for the work of others, and be able to share that work across time. While it will not have the same look and feel of a printed anthology— and I am not advocating that we totally abandon print anthologies either, as there are new self-publishing websites, which I discuss at the end of this chapter, that can make the process easier—a wiki anthology can help students share their work, comment on the work of others, and develop their sense of what to write and revise for a particular audience.

How to Make Class Anthologies with Wikis

Of course, digital writers can and should engage in multimedia authoring whenever possible, so adding images, videos, and hyperlinks to a wiki text can be a useful rhetorical option. And most wikis now make it easy to embed multimedia. For this example, however, I am assuming that most of the digital writing that will be created on the wiki will be text based; that is, students will be using the wiki pages primarily to share the word-processed writing that they have done.

These instructions assume that you have already created a wiki and have some basic familiarity with how they work. Refer back to the section on setting up a wiki in Chapter 3 if necessary. As with the previous blog example, you can use other wiki services such as PBworks or Wetpaint to create the type of anthology I describe here, but the exact layout and functions of the wiki may be slightly different. Additionally, Google Sites can now be configured for multiple users to contribute content, so, while technically not a wiki, it too could be used to create a class anthology. Two teachers that have been mentioned previously, Aram Kabodian and Heather Lewis, share their work through PBworks and Google Sites, respectively, at akabodian7.pbworks.com/ and sites.google.com/site/mrslewisland. My example uses a Wikispaces wiki and you can see examples of how I invite students to create their own pages with their writing at: eng315.wikispaces.com/Student_Wiki_Pages.

1. Create a table of contents page for the anthology.
   a. In your wiki, create a new page. Title it something descriptive, such as **First_Hour_Class_Anthology**. I usually put underscore marks between words so that the page name looks clear in the URL bar; otherwise the wiki will automatically save it with plus symbols or other markers for the spaces and, in my opinion, make the title look awkward.
   b. Create a list of student names. If you are able to simply copy student names from your electronic grade book, that makes things much easier; otherwise, you will have to type them in. I put only my students' first names, and you will need to be aware of your school's policy on how students are able to be identified. Also, I usually make an unordered (bulleted) list so that names do not get combined when students go in to edit the page later. (See Figure 5.4.)
   c. Save your changes and put a hyperlink to the anthology page on your wiki's main page or side navigation bar. To do this, return to the main page or navigation page and edit it to include text linking to your table of contents page. Then, select that text, and create the hyperlink by selecting the Link button and choosing the Existing Wiki Page radio button and the table of contents page from that list.
2. Have each student create her own page.
   a. Once students have become members of the wiki space, invite them to each create their own new page. Again, the title should be descriptive, so if you have multiple students with the same first name, they may have to include a last initial.

FIGURE 5.4

A table of contents page for a class anthology in Wikispaces

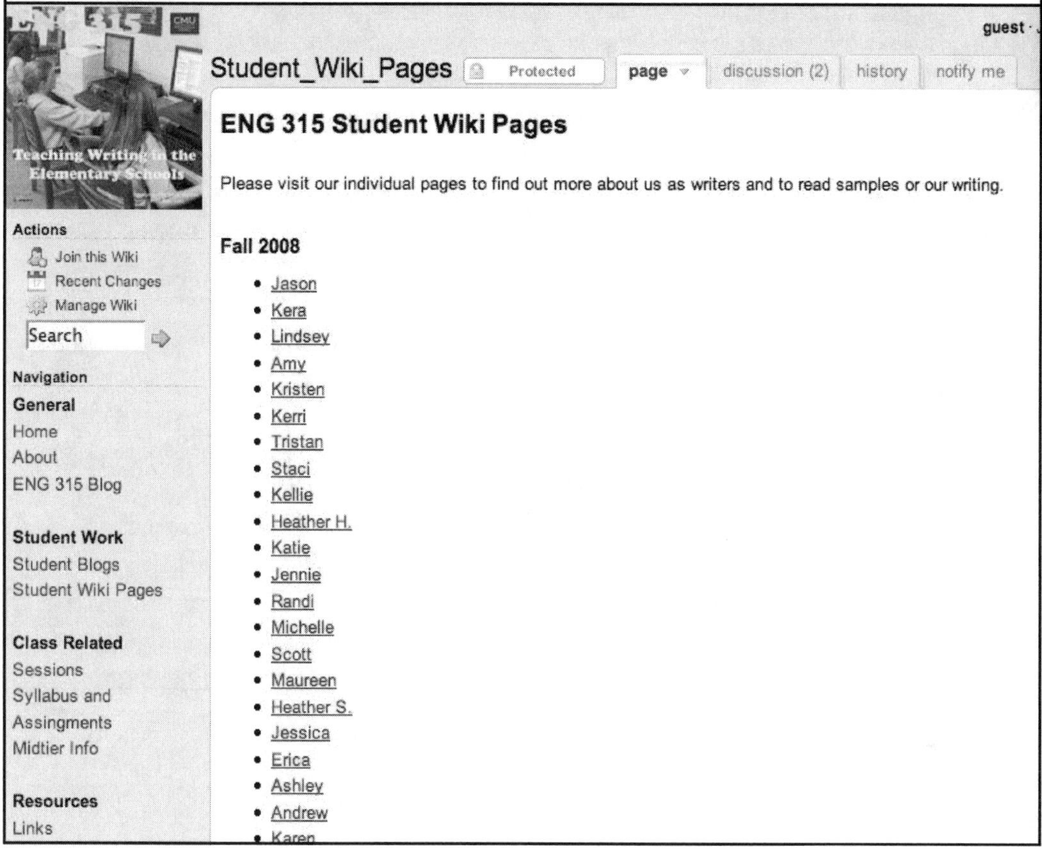

guest ·

Student_Wiki_Pages 🔒 Protected   **page** ▾ discussion (2) history notify me

ENG 315 Student Wiki Pages

Please visit our individual pages to find out more about us as writers and to read samples or our writing.

Fall 2008

- Jason
- Kera
- Lindsey
- Amy
- Kristen
- Kerri
- Tristan
- Staci
- Kellie
- Heather H.
- Katie
- Jennie
- Randi
- Michelle
- Scott
- Maureen
- Heather S.
- Jessica
- Erica
- Ashley
- Andrew
- Karen

Actions
- 🔓 Join this Wiki
- 📑 Recent Changes
- ⚙ Manage Wiki

Search ⇨

Navigation

General
Home
About
ENG 315 Blog

Student Work
Student Blogs
Student Wiki Pages

Class Related
Sessions
Syllabus and
Assingments
Midtier Info

Resources
Links

Teaching Writing in the Elementary Schools

b. On this new page, you can invite students to do a number of things. For instance, I typically have my students do a writing interview with one another (Atwell 1998) and then write up a short bio of their partner. The partner can post this to the other student's page. Also, you might take a digital picture of each student and invite her to embed that image on her page, too. (See Figure 5.5.)

c. Students can add initial content to their page and also create their own table of contents by adding links to new pieces as they are developed.

d. Finally, students should return to the main table of contents page and create a link to their page. One caveat here: students should do this one at a time over the course of the class period, because if they do it

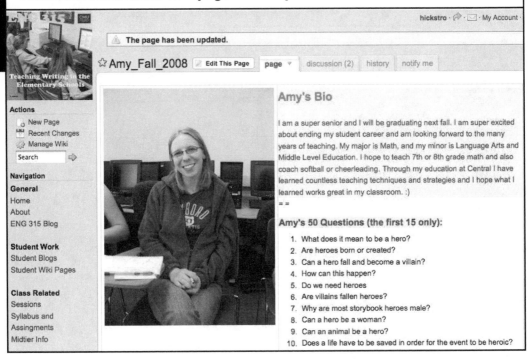

FIGURE 5.5

A student's individual wiki page in Wikispaces

simultaneously from different computers, they can overwrite each other's edits in the wiki page.

3. Over the course of the semester, have students post new work on additional pages and comment on the work of others. As students develop their own pieces and collaborate with peers to both create new writing and revise their own work, they can take advantage of two key wiki features: the Discussion and History tabs.

a. In the Discussion tab, writers can pose questions and state challenges that they are having with their writing so that peers can better focus their responses. Again, employing the bless, address, and press model will help focus responses, too. This initial post will develop a threaded discussion, and the writer can see all the comments from his peers over time. (See Figure 5.6.)

b. In the History tab, the writer can literally see the changes to the individual page over time. As it becomes time to create a final portfolio and reflect on their writing and revising, students can examine the different revisions and use them to discuss their improvements. While it is possible to track changes in a word-processing document over time,

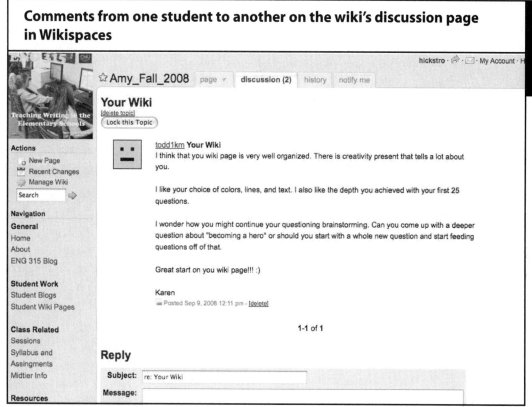

Comments from one student to another on the wiki's discussion page in Wikispaces

FIGURE 5.6

the wiki does this tracking automatically, and students can access those revisions easily.

Thus, when creating a class anthology on a wiki, you are orchestrating the work of all the digital writers in your classroom. Unlike the print anthology, where a student has the potential to dash off a quick piece the day it is due, hand it to the editors, and then not have to participate fully in the writing community, the wiki makes the student's work—both her individual writing as well as her responses given to others—more public. In one sense, of course, this holds students more accountable. In another, more important sense, from my own experience and in talking with other teachers about how wikis work in their classrooms, this type of consistent and recursive process of writing, responding, and revising leads students to become better writers. And, unlike an anthology sitting on a shelf, a wiki is easily searchable so students can look up their peers' work based on the particular person, a title they may remember, or simply a word. And then they can begin reading, responding, and continuing their writing process.

Audio Anthologies

Building on the idea of sharing students' stories through a print anthology, an audio anthology, similar to an audiobook, allows us to literally share students' voices. Creating an audio anthology is, at its most basic, simply recording students as they read their work and transferring those recordings to an audio CD for distribution. These recordings can, of course, become more complex with added music, sound effects, and interludes between students' pieces, yet they do not have to be.

Many students with whom I have worked reported that the process of recording and hearing their voices (and, in many cases rerecording to get a better take) opened both their eyes and their ears. Since the written word and spoken word are different, the process of writing a piece with the intention of recording it can change a writer's perspective on how to punctuate, emphasize, and otherwise engage the listener in ways that seeing his words on paper alone cannot (Reed and Hicks 2009). Thus, creating an audio anthology of student work offers you as a teacher and students as digital writers the opportunity to think differently about the writing process and then share their writing in a way that many students have not experienced.

As with most digital writing, there are multiple ways to go about creating an audio anthology. Two choices that you will have to make immediately involve software and hardware. In terms of hardware, you will need to have digital recorders or microphones for your computers. In terms of the software, you will need a recording tool, such as Audacity (as described in Chapter 3), and a media player capable of creating playlists and burning CDs, such as Apple's iTunes, Microsoft's Windows Media Player, or the open-source VLC media player (www.videolan.org/). Depending on the hardware you have available as well as access to your computer for installing software (or having it installed for you at your school), you'll have many choices to make in terms of the recording process. Thinking about software and hardware will help you determine the best ways to go about creating your anthology in an efficient manner.

First, in terms of the software, there are multiple kinds of media players available, and for this example I have chosen iTunes not only because it is free but because it is available for both Mac and PC platforms. Other players work just as well, and in similar fashion, and you may be limited by your school's acceptable use policy as to what you can and cannot use. As with all digital writing tasks, think about the steps involved in the process of creating an audio anthology and try not to get bogged down with one particular tool, even though I must choose one here for sake of example.

Second, I do not outline the specific steps that it takes to capture students' voices digitally. For a review of that, it may be useful to return to some of the online tutorials mentioned in Chapter 3 about how to record with Audacity created by Chris Sloan (www.judgememorial.com/sloan/audacity/). Also, you can use a digital voice recorder to capture students' voices and you should follow the instructions that came with your recorder in order to get the best quality and correct type of file. Recorders that save files in a more compatible format, such as WAV, are best. For the example shown here, iTunes can import a number of file formats, but not WMA, for instance. Depending on the media player that you choose and the format from the digital recorder itself, this will vary. But, if necessary, you can convert files using a service such as Zamzar (www.zamzar.com/).

Again, the point with this digital writing activity—and with all other forms of digital writing—is that we do not get caught up in the tools. Yes, we need to know the general steps, and that is why I provide an outline here. Yet understanding the larger concepts of how, as well as why, to record, import, and manage audio is more important than knowing how to use every specific tool down to the final detail. When in doubt, ask your students for their help and insight to problem solve and troubleshoot.

How to Make Audio Anthologies with Apple's iTunes

1. Record students reading their work. This can be done formally, where students move to a quiet space and have individual time to record themselves reading. Or it can happen informally during a whole-class read-around or while selected students share in the author's chair. Either way, utilize the recording tool of choice: a digital voice recorder or a microphone connected to a computer using Audacity, as described in Chapter 3 and in the online tutorials mentioned earlier. In either case, when students begin recording, I ask them to state their name and the title of the piece that they are reading, both for my own benefit as an audio editor and so listeners can know who is reading without constantly referring back to the track list.

   a. *Digital recorders*: When possible, have students start and stop the recorder for their story, even if you are doing a read-around for the entire class. This will create individual sound files that will be easier to go back to later and edit. Following the instructions for your recorder, transfer all the audio files onto your computer.

b. *Using Audacity*: Again, have students create individual files for easier exporting and editing. Files can be exported in MP3 or WAV format, and you will need to have them saved in that format, as iTunes (or any other media player) will not be able to read the Audacity project (.aup) files. Please note that Audacity needs to have the LAME MP3 encoder installed, too, in order to export to MP3. Again, instructions can be found online through digitalwritingworkshop.ning.com/.

2. Import into iTunes.

   a. Within iTunes, go to the File menu and select Add to Library to find your files and import them into iTunes.

   b. Once your files are imported, you should see them in your iTunes library.

3. Set up artists, track titles, and album name.

   a. This step is helpful, as it will allow you to go back and easily search for your tracks later as well as to organize your playlist quickly. In Figure 5.7, you will see the contextual menu that appears on a track when doing a right-click (PC) or Control+click (Mac).

   b. Select Get Info and select the Info tab, as shown in Figure 5.8.

   c. Under this tab, you can change the title, artist, album, and other aspects of the track. For your anthology, you will want to make sure that your students' names are listed (or, if required by your school, only their first names) as well as the titles of their pieces of writing and an album name that you will use to connect all the tracks.

   d. Make sure that the information is accurate for all the tracks that you want to include in your anthology. Remember, a typical CD holds approximately seventy-five minutes' worth of audio, so you will want to plan accordingly to have your students record an appropriate amount of material. Thus, in a class of twenty-five, students would be limited to no more than three minutes each if you wanted to keep the anthology to one CD.

4. Create an intro or outro.

   a. If you choose, it is sometimes effective to have a brief intro track that you record to introduce the anthology. These tracks can be as simple or elaborate as you choose. In some anthologies, I have heard students create multivoice tracks or incorporate sound effects. Or, as is the case in the anthology I created in this example, you can simply use a song

The contextual menu for a track in iTunes

FIGURE 5.7

from www.freeplaymusic.com/ which I used as background music for the intro and as a musical piece to end the collection. Ideally, both the intro and the final track contribute to the overall sense of the anthology, much like an illustration on the cover of a printed anthology might.

5. Create a playlist.

   a. In the Search box in the upper right-hand corner of iTunes, do a search for the album name that you just used for your anthology. This should then bring up only the items that you want to use to create a playlist.

   b. Highlight all the tracks by clicking on the top one, then holding down the Shift key and clicking on the bottom one.

FIGURE 5.8

The Info tab, showing information about the track title, artist name, and album name in iTunes

c. In the File menu, select New Playlist from Selection. (See Figure 5.9.)

d. Once the playlist is created, open it up using the navigation bar on the left-hand side of iTunes. Arrange the tracks in the order that you want them to play by dragging files into the proper order.

e. Once your playlist is set, you will see the option of Burn Disc appear in the lower right-hand corner of iTunes. Insert a blank CD and click that button to begin the recording process.

f. Finally, while still in your playlist, choose Print from the File menu. This will allow you to print a jewel case insert or a list of songs that can be distributed with the CDs.

FIGURE 5.9

Creating a playlist in iTunes

As with a class wiki anthology, creating an audio anthology helps strengthen the community in a digital writing workshop and holds students accountable. In my experience as a teacher and researcher, when I have talked to digital writers who have shared their voices through the creation of audio recordings, they talked intently about the ways in which the process of writing, recording, revising, and rerecording made them more conscious of their decision-making process as writers. Besides having the final product to share with your students and beyond your classroom, this intentional stance that they must take as digital writers and speakers is a good enough reason for me to continue using audio anthologies in my teaching.

Some Final Thoughts About Publishing Digital Writing

Based on my own experience and many conversations with teachers, students, and scholars of digital writing, there are two quick caveats about publishing student work that I want to reiterate here. The first is about copyright; the second is about safety.

Despite the broad latitude with which students can transform work, understanding fair use is important for students, as they will be creating and publishing their own work and will want to understand the legal and intellectual ramifications of using copyrighted material. As mentioned in Chapter 1, my thinking on copyright continues to expand as resources such as the Center for Social Media's *Code of Best Practices in Fair Use for Media Literacy Education* (2008) are released. Even with the possibility of transforming copyrighted works under fair-use provisions, when gathering resources for creating digital writing such as images, audio, and video, many of the educators with whom I work, such as Paul Allison, Susan Ettenheim, and Chris Sloan of Youth Voices (youthvoices.net/), ask their students to use materials licensed through Creative Commons (creativecommons.org/). By using Creative Commons work, students can build off the work of others and know that their use of the work is permitted. So, while fair use can allow students certain options as they learn how to express themselves through digital writing, utilizing works that are licensed as Creative Commons, royalty free, or public domain is certainly a route they can take to ensure the work they are building off was meant to be used in that manner. For a list of such resources, visit the book's companion site: digitalwritingworkshop.ning.com/.

Second, I want to reiterate the idea of safety and having a closed community, as that is certainly a question on the minds of many educators, parents, and administrators. Blogs and wikis can be protected so that only authorized users can change and view them. Audio anthologies, once they are released, cannot be easily called back, but limiting the amount of information (such as students' names, grade, and school) can help keep that information more private, if not anonymous. These things said, a key component of teaching digital writing is helping students understand how their work can be distributed, both with their permission and without it; students have to understand how posting anything online or through other digital media will reflect on them, their school, their family, and their communities. So, in making the choice to keep digital portfolios, wiki anthologies, or audio anthologies more or less public, consider the legitimate concerns about student safety but also include discussions with them about how their digital writing could and, most likely, will be distributed in ways that are beyond their control. Ask them, "What kind of persona do you want represented in your digital writing?" Then, as good writing teachers do, help guide them as they craft pieces that best reflect that persona.

Looking Ahead

In the past few years, the publishing industry has undergone a radical change. No longer do authors (or a group of authors) have to vet their work through an established publisher. Instead, they are able to share their work online in a variety of formats. But what if you still wanted a book in hand? An answer that has emerged is on-demand self-publishing. There are a number of sites that allow you to upload a document, create a custom cover, set the price, and then print it. As these services become easier to use and nearly as affordable as taking a stack of student work down to the teacher's workroom or the local copy shop, they offer students the chance to become "published" authors with the look and feel of a "real" book.

While I know that cost constraints still make these types of options unaffordable in some situations, I mention them here because I think that students need to understand two things about self-publishing. First, the fact that anyone can now publish a book (let alone to his own blog or any of numerous other websites) raises the perennial questions about credibility. One question to ask, for instance, is "Just because a self-published book has a high sales rank with an online bookstore, does that mean it is credible?" Second, and returning to the idea of copyright stated previously, if someone chooses to self-publish, she still needs to be cognizant of the copyright laws that may come into effect by creating and distributing that work. In the case of one friend of mine, she self-published a fan fiction book using characters from an established series of books. Yet, knowing the consequences, she printed only about a dozen copies and distributed them to her fan fiction writing group personally. Copyright violation? I am not a lawyer, but I believe it could be stretching the limits of fair use even though she transformed the use of the characters. Yet, in her eyes, it was an ethical way to extend her passion for writing about characters that she enjoyed reading about. Also, consider that, in other countries, such as Japan with its manga, breaking copyright law is a part of the culture of that kind of writing, as fan fiction is sold right alongside original texts (Pink 2007).

So, while the landscape of digital writing can be confusing to navigate from these legal and ethical standpoints, it clearly is a part of the remix culture in which we now live and students will have to learn to compose. Perhaps even more pertinent for teachers of writing are the trickier questions about how to assess students' digital writing, the topic of Chapter 6. As with traditional writing, there are no surefire ways to assess digital writing; yet by examining the processes and products in thoughtful ways, we can adapt our formative and summative assessments to meet the needs of our digital writers.

Enabling Assessment over Time with Digital Writing Tools

6

An ever-present difficulty in teaching students to write is measuring the growth that they are making from day to day, semester to semester, and year to year. Teachers now have the opportunity to watch and guide students' writing through many of the technologies mentioned heretofore in the book, and this chapter looks at them through the lens of assessment. For instance, teachers can track drafts of a student's work, along with commentary on that work from other students, with an online word processor. By tagging blog posts on a particular topic, students can track their own thinking—and the quality of their writing—over time. Keeping in mind what good writers do (Burke 2003) and the six plus one traits (Northwest Regional Educational Laboratory 2005; Spandel 2005), teachers can formatively and summatively assess students while leading them through their own self-assessment and reflection using digital writing tools.

Our Trouble with Assessing Digital Writing

Here's a brief story to outline the challenge of assessing digital writing. When I was a middle school language arts teacher, students in their nine-week computer class were generally introduced to the basic functions of an office suite and expected to produce a document, spreadsheet, and presentation that integrated content from their other classes. This was a pedagogically thoughtful move on the part of the computer teacher, in that it invited students to learn about the programs for multiple purposes, such as to track heart rates in physical education, write a research paper for social studies, or, for my class, create a presentation about themselves as individuals and as writers for a community-building exercise in the writing workshop.

The problem came when students got one vision of assessment in their computer class and another in mine. Specifically, the computer teacher was mostly concerned about how many slides were in the presentation, each having a particular purpose (e.g., my name, my family, what I like, etc.) with a certain number of images, fonts, colors, backgrounds, transitions, and other effects enabled by the slide show program. I do not have to explain what happened, as I am sure you are picturing all my seventh graders, each presenting a slide show that was, at best visually and organizationally incoherent and, at worst, simply gaudy. Watching all of these slide shows made for a few long days, but it taught me that the process and product of digital writing, like all writing, are intricately intertwined. And, in turn, the assessment of digital writing must be, too.

While I purposely embellished this story just a bit, and I hold no hard feelings toward my colleague, who was, at the time, asking the students to complete tasks that were laid out in the district's technology curriculum guidelines, what I do want to mention is the fact that we often miss the point with assessment, especially with assessment of digital writing. It is important that students do have a basic understanding of different programs and how those programs are used. Formatting text, inserting pictures, creating graphs, and making hyperlinks are important skills. Yet starting with the programs, and not with the task of digital writing itself, causes us to miss the point. What are we assessing, exactly? The number of slides? Fonts? Colors used? Instead, we need to assess the quality of the information on those slides as well as the ways in which the entire slide show is designed, thus leading to an overall aesthetic effect.

Therefore, the tools themselves should not be the focus of the assessment. Rather, we need to begin thinking about what it means to assess the process and products of digital writing, using means that are both formative and summative. By thinking through all the angles of assessment from the beginning of teaching a topic all the way to evaluating the final product, we can enable our students to both grow as digital writers and produce excellent pieces of digital writing. I do not pretend to have all the answers about assessment, and I recommend that you review scholars such as Wiggins and McTighe (2005), who offer frameworks for thinking about assessment, as well as the numerous other English educators who discuss assessment in more detail than I will here (Broad

2003; Cooper and Odell 1999; Strickland and Strickland 1998), as well as those who write about portfolio assessment (Belanoff and Dickson 1991; Yagelski 1997; Yancey and Weiser 1997), alternative assessments (Tchudi and NCTE Committee on Alternatives to Grading Student Writing 1997), and standardized assessments (Gere, Christenbury, and Sassi 2005). Thus, I offer just a brief examination of assessment practices in teaching writing to frame this chapter.

Examining Assessment

Writing teachers look at a variety of aspects of student performance to develop a complete assessment of their work as writers. To introduce the topic and contextualize what we understand about assessing both the process and the product of writing, I will touch on only a few key ideas written about assessment. NCTE suggests that "assessment must include multiple measures and must be manageable" (2004); thus, we will explore how digital writing tools can help students and teachers engage in these multiple, manageable measures of assessing students' digital writing processes and products. To do so, we will examine ways to incorporate discussions of digital writing into the formative and summative stages of assessment, noting that instruction and assessment are intertwined and that digital writing makes that relationship even more complicated.

First, a brief discussion of assessment as it relates to the teaching of writing in general. As noted earlier, a number of scholars have dedicated their careers to researching writing assessments and, as teachers, we know that we certainly spend a great deal of time in the act of assessing our student writers. We assess, ideally, on both process and product, thus bringing our relationships with our students into play with our evaluation of their writing. While we recognize that there are times when focusing only on the product is necessary, students ought to be rewarded for "diligence *and* for the quality of writing that they produce" in that "[t]here can be a set of performance goals which might include expectations for types of writing to be attempted, for revision, for participation in response groups, for meeting deadlines, and for self-assessment" (Newkirk and Kent 2007, 65).

This judgment of process and product happens, then, through the act of formative and summative assessment. Formative writing assessments include "commenting on drafts, soliciting peer response, and holding writing conferences" whereas summative writing assessments are "a letter grade on a final essay or portfolio, or a standardized test score" (NCTE 2008). In both cases, and as evidenced in a variety of professional publications spanning the range of literacy learning from early childhood into adulthood, the community of writing teachers and scholars has come to realize the value of assessing both process and product, through methods that are both formative and summative.

In this line of thinking, then, I have chosen to frame this chapter around the notion of formative and summative assessment. And, while it may be artificial to divide the two types of assessments in this manner, I generally refer to formative assessment as happening during the *process* of digital writing while summative assessment happens after the process, focusing more on the *product*. This is not an entirely clear distinction, as one could argue that a final portfolio is just as much a formative assessment of the writer as it is a summative assessment of the writing itself. And some even note the tension inherent in our times where we are struggling to integrate newer literacies and technologies into a paradigm of assessment that seems, well, antiquated:

> At the same time that new forms of writing—and thus literacy—are emerging in our culture and in our classrooms, forces of assessment and standardization exert a counter-pressure, asking us to prepare students to produce conventional, formulaic print texts in scripted ways. Paradoxically, technology is also being harnessed for these purposes by educational publishers and testing companies, taking the form of machine-scoring and responding to student writing. So it is that technology seems to be leading us forward to new forms of writing, but, as used by standardized testing programs, backward to the five-paragraph theme. (Herrington and Moran 2009, 2)

Teaching in a digital writing workshop means that we teach students to compose using newer literacies and technologies, not that we simply use technologies that assess traditional modes of writing and reply only to traditional measures such as having an obvious thesis statement with adequate supporting details. Instead, we need to teach digital writers to assess their work through a series of decisions that hold true to the idea that writers need authentic audiences and purposes, need to write in varied genres, and need to reflect upon their work.

Moreover, as noted throughout this book, digital spaces complicate how and why writers share their work. Perhaps this type of digital writing forces students to do certain types of identity work that simply producing texts on paper did not ask:

[W]hat we ask students to do is who we ask them to be. As important, these representations constitute a rhetorical situation, precisely (1) because they are immediate, direct, and substantive—composing, as they do, the material of our teaching lives and those of our students'— and (2) because they perform a double function—providing grist for the twin mills of identity and assessment. (Yancey 2004, 739)

In other words, we ask students to create public digital writing personas at the same time they know that they are doing work for a grade. No longer is writing about trying to just please the teacher so as to earn an "A." It is an act of identity formation, a twenty-first-century skill that students need to have as they represent themselves across a variety of online communities. It is a difficult place for us to put our students, and for us to be in as teachers.

That said, there is reason to believe that digital writing can be assessed, both formatively and summatively, and in smart ways. By relying on what we know about formative and summative assessment, and connecting them to some examples from the digital writing tools we have explored in this text, you can make a few minor changes in your writing pedagogy—as enabled by the digital writing tools we have discussed—that will help you teach your students to be more metacognitive about their writing. As discussed in the previous chapter and highlighted throughout the book, when students are writing for real audiences and purposes, there are real reactions and consequences for them as writers (sometimes positive, sometimes negative). If we are thinking about assessment—and what it means to be a digital writer, attempting to meet what was described in Chapter 4 as the MAPS (mode and media, audience, purpose, and situation) of a variety of writing tasks both in and out of school—then these reactions are the real assessment.

So, how can digital writing tools assist our students as well as us in assessment? Before moving into this discussion, remember reports and curricular documents cited in Chapter 4 that outline *twenty-first-century skills, digital literacy, information literacy, media literacy,* and numerous state technology standards. While I do not address those types of standards directly here, I do suggest that you look at them and think about the ways in which your digital writing workshop complements and extends the types of cognitive work and performance tasks that are being asked of students. In asking students to become digital writers, you will also be asking them to become proficient with file management, software interfaces, web searching, participating in online communities, and creating multimedia work—all standards that these documents address to some degree or another.

Terms such as *collaboration, analysis, inquiry, synthesis, critical thinking, flexibility,* and *creativity* permeate the pages of all of these documents. While I cannot fully outline the changes in how educators and other constituencies who produce these documents have come to think about what it means to learn and write in a digital age, suffice it to say that our assessments need to challenge students in ways that we could have barely even imagined before the advent of digital writing. In addition to those documents mentioned before, it is also worth reviewing Bernajean Porter's DigiTales interactive scoring guides for digital media: digitales.us/evaluating/scoring_guide.php. In considering all these resources, and by examining formative and summative approaches for assessing digital writing, we can begin to think more carefully about how to scaffold students into this kind of learning experience.

Formative Assessment of Digital Writing

In exploring what it means to be a writer and how one engages in the writing process, students and teachers participate in formative assessments. As noted previously, these assessments occur when teachers and students confer, when peers give comments on drafts, and when writers discuss their process of writing and revision. Still, formative assessment of digital writing occurs in much the same way as traditional writing pedagogy has—through conversations about writing.

As shown through the examples in this book, digital writing tools allow teachers and students unprecedented access into the writing process. From blog posts that accumulate into a collection of work, to draft upon draft of revisions that are automatically stored in a wiki's history or in an online word processor, students are increasingly able to easily archive and return to their work over time. Thus, the process of formative assessment has become more transparent. As teachers, we can ask students to review drafts of their writing, comment on the writing of others, and reflect on the writing process—and there are (usually) no more lost files to hamper their work. Digital writing tools allow the conversations to continue anytime, anywhere.

So, whether happening in a teacher-student conference, a peer writing group, or through comments left on a blog post or wiki discussion page, these writing conversations help guide writers as they develop their pieces. Beach et al. (2008) offer a number of other strategies for formative evaluation of student writing, including reader-based feedback on blog posts, conference-style synchronous chat sessions, asynchronous feedback via tools such as discussion boards, and inserting comments into a word-processing document. No matter what the tool and the approach, in terms of MAPS, one of the primary tasks of formative assessment is to help writers frame their writing project. To reiterate:

- *Mode and media*: What genre am I attempting to write in and what medium (or media) will help me best convey my message?
- *Audience*: Who is the intended audience? What other audiences might I reach, intentionally or unintentionally?
- *Purpose*: What is my purpose? How does the broad choice of mode and media as well as specific choices about the topic, organization, and even words I use affect my purpose?
- *Situation for the writer and the writing*: What do I know about this topic and the digital writing tool I hope to employ? How much time and training might I need to create this piece of digital writing?

Another interesting way to think about design, and how to create pieces of digital writing, comes from Robin Williams and her *Non-Designer's Design Book* (2008). In this text, she outlines four principles of design:

1. *Contrast*: creating visual elements such as type, color, and shape that are very different from one another so as to have them stand out in the text
2. *Repetition*: using the visual elements multiple times in effective manners to organize the text
3. *Alignment*: visually connecting every element of the text with real or imagined lines
4. *Proximity*: grouping elements together that are related in order to organize information in the text

These four principles can help digital writers structure the visual elements of their texts so that they have the maximum effect on the viewer or reader.

Design, then, is an essential component of digital writing. For instance, the Writing in Digital Environments Research Collective, in its article "Why Teach Digital Writing?" (2005), argues that "[w]riting isn't just scripting text anymore. Writing requires carefully and critically analyzing and selecting among multiple media elements." During the process of formative assessment, digital writing teachers help their students do this careful and critical analysis. Keeping this principle, as well as these broad questions from MAPS, in mind, teachers can focus on more specific traits to consider for digital writing, which build on a set of traits articulated by teacher and author Jim Burke in his book *Writing Reminders* (2003).

Effective and Ineffective Digitial Writers

Jim Burke presents "traits of effective and ineffective writers" (2003, 189), clearly outlining what it means to be a successful academic writer, and compares what each type of writer does before, during, and after writing. For instance, before writing, an effective writer will "[i]dentify the type of text or genre so [he] know[s] how to write it" (189) whereas an ineffective writer will "[t]reat texts equally, writing them without consideration of audience, conventions, or voice" (189). This list is an effective tool to share with your writers, especially at the beginning of the year when establishing your writing workshop and when students are reflecting on their writing process.

Moreover, when thinking about the specific ways in which digital writers need to work, there are a few additional traits that will help guide you and your students through the writing process. With permission from Burke, I have copied his list in Figure 6.1 and expanded upon his ideas as they relate to digital writing. This is not a complete list of traits that you might discuss during formative assessments of digital writing, yet it should help you begin thinking about the *kinds* of questions that you can ask your digital writers before, during, and after the writing process. I suggest sharing this list at the beginning of your writing workshop, most likely at the start of the school year or new semester, and return to it often while students are reflecting on their digital writing process.

FIGURE 6.1

Traits of effective and ineffective digital writers

Effective Writers	Ineffective Writers
Before You Write	
• Determine what you already know and need to learn. • Read the directions. • Establish a purpose or a question you are trying to answer through your writing. • Ask others—classmates or the teacher—if you do not understand what you are supposed to do.	• Begin writing without asking yourself what you know or need to learn. • Ignore or barely look at the directions. • Do not establish a purpose or, because you did not read the directions, establish an incorrect purpose: write with no question to answer. • Do not ask for help.

Traits of effective and ineffective digital writers (continued)

FIGURE 6.1

Effective Writers	Ineffective Writers
Before You Write	

Effective Writers	Ineffective Writers
• Gather any tools, ideas, or materials you might need and determine how best to use them.	• Lack the tools, ideas, or materials that would help you be an effective, informed writer.
• Provide a quiet, studious environment in which to think, read, and write.	• Try to work in an environment filled with distractions.
• Establish appropriate and reasonable goals for the assignment, taking into consideration the demands of the text, your personal writing goals, and the time needed to write this particular text.	• Do not evaluate the demands or difficulties of your writing assignments. You just jump in and start writing without a goal or purpose in mind.
• Identify the type of text or genre so you know how to write it.	• Treat texts equally, writing them without consideration of audience, conventions, or voice.
• Generate ideas using a range of strategies: these ideas involve not only the subject but strategies you will use to write about it.	• Make no effort or do not know how to generate ideas about a topic.

Additional Aspects to Consider Before Writing Digitally

- *Choosing media*: Select an appropriate digital writing tool for the given task based on your needs for privacy, response, and interaction with other writers. This tool may be text only or may be multimedia or web based.
- *Understanding copyright*: If creating your own new content, begin your design process with the intent of obeying copyright laws. Either aim to make transformative use of the work under fair use provisions, or find copyright-free, public domain, or Creative Commons–licensed materials that can be reused legally.
- *Citing sources*: If reporting on or integrating existing content, search for and integrate materials conscientiously, following proper citation styles. Use social bookmarking or a tool such as Zotero (www.zotero.org/) to keep track of sources.
- *File management*: Create an appropriate file management system either through the use of web-based accounts such as Dropbox (www.getdropbox.com/) that can be accessed at home, school, or elsewhere or by saving materials in a commonly accessible format on a portable media drive. Maintain regular updates of drafts of documents.
- *Planning*: Develop outlines, storyboards, cluster maps, or other appropriate texts, especially when creating multimedia texts, that provide an overview of the project so as to plan accordingly and gather digital resources.
- *Collaboration*: Choose digital writing tools that invite appropriate kinds of collaboration from peers, teacher, and outside audiences (e.g., posting to a blog if wanting general feedback as compared with posting in a collaborative word processor for line-by-line comments).

(continues)

FIGURE 6.1

Traits of effective and ineffective digital writers (continued)

Effective Writers	Ineffective Writers
While You Write	

Effective Writers	Ineffective Writers
• Continually check what you write against the assignment, the text about which you are writing, and the question you are trying to answer through your writing.	• Never or rarely check the topic of the text about which you are writing; you charge on, more concerned with finishing than doing it correctly or well.
• Check for understanding as you write; if you get lost, you use various strategies to help you understand. You are a reflective, recursive writer.	• Pay no attention to whether you understand what you are writing about; if you get lost you do not use some strategies to help you get unstuck.
• Make connections between what you are writing and your own experience and knowledge.	• Do not make any connections; you may not see what you are reading as related to yourself or anything else.
• Ask questions to help you generate examples, details, or connections.	• Do not ask questions, which results in writing that lacks necessary information and useful examples.
• If writing about a text—that is, poem, book, film, or image—you return to it, rereading it to better understand it and find supporting details for the ideas you explore in your paper.	• If writing about a text, you do not reread it.
• Make notes and generate other possible approaches as you write, checking to see if they would improve the paper you are writing.	• Make no notes; do not consider alternative approaches.
• Evaluate and revise as necessary those essential aspects of effective writing: voice, organization, clarity, ideas, conventions, mechanics.	• Make no effort to evaluate or revise; you just get it down so you have something to turn in.

Additional Aspects to Consider While Writing Digitally

- *Use of digital writing tools*: Choose multimedia, hyperlinks, and other design elements appropriately in order to emphasize the text's rhetorical purpose, to "illuminate" the text (Porter 2009) and not simply for effect.
- *Design*: Incorporate elements of design such as contrast, repetition, alignment, proximity (Williams 2008) throughout the text in order to organize the entire text and articulate specific points, often creating your own designs from scratch or modifying existing designs.
- *Citation*: Clearly and appropriately cite materials, embedding hyperlinks to web-based documents where appropriate.

FIGURE 6.1

Traits of effective and ineffective digital writers (continued)

Effective Writers	Ineffective Writers
• *Collaboration and response*: Invite peers, teachers, and outside audiences to offer response by framing specific questions and time lines for feedback.	

After You Write

Effective Writers	Ineffective Writers
• Check for understanding and success, asking such questions as, Do I understand what I wrote? and Did I achieve my stated purpose in this piece of writing? If necessary, you return to the text or consult others who can help you improve what you wrote. • Reread the topic or assignment so you can be sure you met the requirements. • Edit for clarity. • Edit for correctness. • Reflect on what you did and how you did it so you can learn and do better on future writing assignments.	• Do not check for understanding or consult others if you did not understand the assignment. • Do not revisit the topic; this may keep you from realizing you went off topic. • Do not edit for clarity. • Do not edit for correctness. • Do not reflect on what you did. Make no effort to think about what worked or why.

Additional Aspects to Consider After Writing Digitally

- *Publication and distribution*: Find the most accessible and flexible distribution format and location (e.g., choosing to post a video to a video-sharing site so anyone with a web browser can view an embedded version on your blog as compared with saving it only as a proprietary movie file hyperlinked from a page).
- *Feedback*: Incorporate feedback from peers, teachers, and outside audiences into future versions of the text.
- *Reflection*: Write or discuss principles about digital writing in general or about the particular topic in order to make more informed decisions about how to address MAPS in future work.

   As you examine these traits of your students—and encourage them to ask these questions of themselves about their digital writing processes—their skills and confidence as digital writers will increase. Adopting a stance as an effective writer takes time, and by continuing to think about how he approaches his writing process, a student will begin to make choices about the mode, audience, purpose, and situation, including all the digital dimensions mentioned in Figure 6.1. Once those decisions become a part of the digital writing process, and part of the routine of your digital writing workshop, it is time to move toward summative assessment of student work.

Summative Assessment of Digital Writing

As students move some of their digital writing pieces toward completion, and you need to perform summative assessments of that work, one model for completing that kind of assessment that stands out is the six traits model. Moreover, it is a model with which many teachers are familiar. Since the basic premises behind the development of the six traits model as well as the criteria for the traits themselves are described fully in a number of other sources (see, for instance, Northwest Regional Educational Laboratory 2005; Spandel 2005), I do not offer a full definition of them here except to note that the model builds upon many years of research related to the assessment of key elements, or traits, of a piece of writing: ideas, organization, voice, word choice, sentence fluency, and conventions. In recent years, the six traits rubrics have included one more trait, the "plus one" trait of presentation and/or publication. And, if it is not obvious from the focus of the previous chapter and the book as a whole, studying and evaluating the design and presentation of digital writing is critical. Since the medium that one chooses to create a text dictates to some degree the way in which it is presented or published, this aspect of the work should be articulated clearly as a part of summative assessment.

I offer two caveats here. First, there are many critics of particular kinds of summative assessments, especially standardized tests and an overreliance on rubrics (e.g., Hillocks 2002; Newkirk and Kent 2007; Kohn 2000; Wilson 2006). Six traits can be used in formative and summative assessments to help guide writers toward better writing, but they should not be the only means by which a writer and her writing are judged, especially if the score is based on only one isolated piece of writing. As discussed previously, portfolios provide one of the most robust ways for teachers to assess their writers and, for that matter, for students to self-assess.

Second, the ways in which I describe six traits for digital writing here in Figure 6.2 are not meant to be a rubric in and of themselves, per se; instead, like Figure 6.1, I hope that they help inform you as you make decisions about how to adapt assessments that you might already be using to incorporate elements of digital writing and, moreover, consider the ways in which different media change the ways in which we conceive writing. My aim is that you can use these questions to guide your students during the composing process (thus using them in a formative way) and not just as ways to evaluate their final products. Peter Elbow, through work across his entire career (e.g., Elbow 1998, 2000; Elbow and Belanoff 2003), warns writing teachers that overassessing students not only takes the joy out of teaching writing but also encourages students to think that

FIGURE 6.2

Ideas for applying the six traits to summative assessment of digital writing

	Individual Blogs	Group Wikis	Photo-Essays	Podcasts	Digital Stories
Ideas and organization: the main idea and structure of the piece conveyed through text, hypertext, or multimedia elements, often partially determined by the medium in which it is presented	• Posts are titled and tagged appropriately. • References to other sources are hyperlinked and quoted. • Image, audio, and video files are embedded when appropriate.	• Writers work to create pages that are clear and concise, building on the ideas of others as appropriate. • Revisions show growth over time, incorporating feedback.	• Writers choose images or take their own photographs that show the subject in a unique manner. • The photos are arranged in a manner consistent with the story being told (chronological, focusing inward or outward).	• Given the genre of the podcast, main ideas are presented early enough in the work so as to alert the listener to the topic. • Additional ideas are presented with transitions and, as appropriate, repetition of key ideas.	• Through a combination of spoken voice, background audio and music, and appropriate images and/or video, the story has a compelling theme and clear beginning, middle, and end.
Voice: the persona the writer adopts based on the purpose, audience, and topic	• Writers take a stance appropriate to the topic at hand, moving from personal reflection to more thoughtful analysis on the subject over the course of subsequent blog posts.	• Since the work is written collaboratively, the voice of the piece blends all the coauthors into a coherent whole that has a unified voice and presents the subject in a thorough manner.	• Captions are used judiciously to highlight key elements of the photo. • In capturing different angles on a subject, the photos illustrate it in various ways to show different perspectives.	• Quite literally, the narrator uses her own voice to convey both the words being read and the tone by which they should be interpreted. • Appropriate use of speaking techniques such as inflection, pauses, and repetition should be evident.	• Like a podcast, the digital story literally has the narrator's voice conveying both the story itself and the tone of that story through inflection, pauses, and repetition, as appropriate. Images and transitions contribute to the effect of the spoken voice.

(continues)

FIGURE 6.2

Ideas for applying the six traits to summative assessment of digital writing (continued)

	Individual Blogs	Group Wikis	Photo-Essays	Podcasts	Digital Stories
Word choice, sentence fluency, and conventions: the selection of particular words, sentence structures, and the use of punctuation and grammar for rhetorical effect	• Because this writing is typically presented as an early-draft format, these elements related to more polished writing are not as important as the ideas being expressed, yet the writing must be understandable.	• Given the topic, writers work together to choose appropriate vocabulary and patterns of writing that help blend voices together. • Appropriate vocabulary is chosen for the context of the topic (e.g., literary terminology).	• Because the actual number of written words is small, they are presented well. • Conventional elements of photography including angle, lighting, and focus become an important part of discussing conventions.	• Because this is an audio-only experience, word choice and sentence variety should contribute to the overall effect of the essay. • New terms should be introduced clearly and sentence patterns varied to keep listeners' attention.	• By combining spoken words, written words, and images, the digital story demonstrates a variety of sentence patterns that keep the viewer engaged in the entire multimedia experience.
Presentation or publication: the interaction of content and design for rhetorical effect	• In using the functions of the blog for changing fonts, hyperlinking, and embedding media, the writer makes appropriate decisions about how to balance her own content with that of other effects and sources.	• The final piece is presented as a singular page; sections that have been individually authored follow formatting guidelines and blend together to create a consistent whole.	• As a collection, individual photos and the entire photo-essay evoke a particular mood that conveys an overall effect such as persuading the viewer to take action.	• Combined with background music and sound effects, the narration is compelling and woven together with appropriate pauses to allow for a combined effect on the listener.	• As noted by Porter (2009), the use of media in the digital story "illuminates" the main ideas, thus making it an experience that could not happen with written text alone.

they are writing only for a teacher. By keeping some of the other ideas introduced in this text such as MAPS and William's design principles in mind when integrating the six traits to create your own assessment tools, you'll help your students think about what they need to do to both be effective digital writers as well as earn the grades that they want.

I have outlined and (in the case of ideas and organization and then again with word choice, sentence fluency, and conventions) condensed the six traits into four broad categories for purposes of this discussion. In Figure 6.2, I highlight five of the digital writing tools that have been introduced in this book and suggest ways in which you can consider those traits as you assess student work. Like most of the ideas presented in this text, these are not meant to be concrete expectations that you will use in your digital writing workshop. Instead, these questions and ideas are meant to spark conversations with your students and colleagues about how and why we assess digital writing.

In considering all the aspects of formative and summative assessment of digital writing, we need to account for both the process and the product. Through a collaborative digital writing process, Paul Allison invited a number of colleagues, myself included, to join him in creating the matrix pictured in Figure 6.3 for his students who were learning how to blog. Allison set up the initial matrix with the "Participating," "Producing," "Perfecting," and "Publishing" headings as well as the categories on the side and shared it as a Google Doc with nearly fifty colleagues (http://docs.google.com/Doc?docid=ah5m9qjtkbwf_27mcjg27&hl=en). During the first two years since its inception, the document underwent nearly five hundred revisions. Of course, not all fifty people made changes, and many of the revisions were made by Allison as he adapted the matrix for different classes, but many users contributed to the overall design of the assessment. For instance, my contribution was to adapt a technique that I had seen used in expository writing classes called "the three ins": introduce, insert, and interpret. Others added links, asked questions, or simply revised for clarity. Over time, the assessment has become more robust and helps capture both what digital writers do in the process of blogging as well as what their final product should look like. Allison (2009, 75) suggests that engaging in these tasks invites his students to become "passionate self-guided learners who seek to improve their skills to keep up with and impress their peers." Isn't this one of the goals for any kind of assessment—to lead students into independence? As we think about what it means to assess digital writing in both formative and summative ways, I argue that this type of matrix could be adapted and used to describe nearly every kind of writing discussed in this book. I look forward to seeing how you make these adaptations and hope that you share them on the book's companion site: digitalwritingworkshop.ning.com/.

FIGURE 6.3

An example of a formative and summative assessment tool for digital writing: the Be a Blogger! matrix

BE A BLOGGER!

Follow all sixteen of these each week.   Name _____

	Participating (Responding)	Producing (Drafting)	Perfecting (Revising and Editing)	Publishing
Text	Read and listen to posts by other students in your class or *Community*, or on *Your Friends* list. *Add a comment* in two of their blogs. Keep focused on the content of that post, not how it is written. Be sure to quote two times from his or her post. Remember to introduce, insert, and interpret.	1. Pose a good question for yourself. Make this the title for a document in Google Docs. *Freewrite* for 10 or 15 minutes. 2. Write a *Focused Sentence*, a perfectly written, opinionated sentence that restates your entire freewrite. *Freewrite* again, this time starting with the *Focused Sentence*. Write 5+ tags for this doc.	Copy your text to Microsoft Word and check grammar (green) and spelling (red). Revise your freewriting. – Delete unnecessary words + Add more details. <-> Rearrange sentences and paragraphs ?! Replace slang or confusing words. Look to see that you are adding to the conversation.	After you have finished correcting everything in Word, copy back to your Google Docs, then copy the Google Docs file to your blog. Be sure you have: 1. good title 2. 5+ tags 3. set Access to Public, unless told otherwise

(Courtesy of Paul Allison; used with permission.)

FIGURE 6.3

An example of a formative and summative assessment tool for digital writing: the Be a Blogger! matrix (continued)

	Participating (Responding)	Producing (Drafting)	Perfecting (Revising and Editing)	Publishing
Image	Search for Creative Commons images using these sites: • flickr.com/creative commons/by-nc-nd-2.0 • Stock.xchng: sxc.hu • morgueFile • Wikimedia Commons • flickrcc.bluemountains.net/ • (see more)	Insert a *Creative Commons* image or one of your own. Remember to introduce, insert, and interpret. 3. *Freewrite* for a third time, this time with the image in mind. How does it represent what you are trying to get across in your post?	At the bottom of your post, write: Image Source: 1. "Title," 2. Name or ID of Photo-grapher, 3. link to this photo online	Align your photograph left or right—and give it some horizontal and vertical space—so that the text wraps around. Images should be no larger than 250 pixels wide.

(continues)

(Courtesy of Paul Allison; used with permission.)

FIGURE 6.3

An example of a formative and summative assessment tool for digital writing: the Be a Blogger! matrix (continued)

	Participating (Responding)	Producing (Drafting)	Perfecting (Revising and Editing)	Publishing
Links	Read blogs, news, and websites. Subscribe, then find blog posts and news items in your Google Reader subscriptions list. Read and copy *Snippets* or quotations. Also use Delicious to collect websites to use in your blog. Bookmark and tag web pages. Quote from these.	Add two *Snippets* or quotations from other blogs or news items that you have read—or podcasts you have listened to—about this topic. 4. *Freewrite* a final time with these quotations in mind. Remember to introduce, insert, and interpret. How does each quote add to your message in your post?	Make hyperlinks to the *Snippets* or quotations that you have included in your post. If you use the clipboard in Flock, the links will be automatically inserted for you.	Use highlighted *Keywords* from the bottom of one of your posts, from your list of *Tags*, or from *Your Profile* to find someone with similar interests or blog posts. Add this person to *Your Friends* list, and *Add a comment* to his or her related blog post.

(Courtesy of Paul Allison; used with permission.)

FIGURE 6.3

An example of a formative and smmative assessment tool for digital writing: the Be a Blogger! matrix (continued)

	Participating (Responding)	Producing (Drafting)	Perfecting (Revising and Editing)	Publishing
Podcasts	Use Google Reader to listen to selected podcasts that you have subscribed to. Use Podzinger to find more audio and video about topics of interest. In Google Docs, write comments about these podcasts with links to the original source. Use Podcast Sentence Starters.	Use Audacity to record. Be sure to introduce yourself with your first name and say the name of your school. Explain what you are about to read. It's OK to say more than what is in your post, but not less. Export it as an MP3, saving it to your folder.	Upload your MP3 to a "Podcast" folder in your *My Files*. In the description box for your MP3, copy the first sentence from your blog, then type "read more," and make this into a link to your blog post. See How to set up your podcast files.	Embed your MP3 file from your elgg storage using the *Add* button at the bottom of your post. A small player should appear in your post.

Introduce, Insert, Interpret

- *Introduce* the quote or photograph. Begin with something about what the blogger said or describe the photograph with something like "I noticed…"
- *Insert* the quote or photograph. Use quotation marks or block quote in HTML.
- *Interpret* the quote or photograph. Why do you think the blogger said this or the photographer took a picture like this? What are your thoughts on it?

Adding to the Conversation

Did you
- Add a new idea to the conversation, pointing to a new resource or another blogger?
- Ask a new question that could further the conversation in productive ways?

(continues)

(Courtesy of Paul Allison; used with permission.)

FIGURE 6.3

An example of a formative and summative assessment tool for digital writing: the Be a Blogger! matrix (continued)

Podcast Sentence Starters

Dear <Podcaster's Name>:

- What I noticed most about "<Exact Title of the Episode><Add a link to the original source MP3 under your title.>" was <…Add two or three sentences describing what stands out for you>. When you said, "<Quote from the podcast.>," I was thinking <Report what was going on in your head the first time you heard this part of the podcast.>. I think this is < _____ (descriptive adjective)> because <…Add one or two sentences explaining why you chose this quote.>.
- Another part that I <_____ (strong verb)> was "<Quote from the podcast or news item.>." This stood out for me because <…Add one or two sentences.>.
- I <do/don't _____ly (adverb)> agree with you that <…Summarize something from the podcast that you have an opinion about.>. One reason I say this is <…Explain in one or two sentences.>. Another reason I <agree/disagree> with you is <…Give another reason in a couple of sentences.>.
- <End your response in a nice way, by thanking the podcaster for his or her work and saying why you might want to hear more from this young podcaster. Why might you want to his or her thoughts again in the future?>

In order to create a basic podcast as an MP3 file that you upload to the internet, you will need to have the free Audacity software (*audacity.sourceforge.net*) downloaded and installed on your computer, including the LAME MP3 encoder (*lame.buanzo.com.ar/*). Follow the instructions on these pages to download and install the software. This brief tutorial also assumes that you are using Edublogs as your service for hosting your podcast, although posting your podcast to other websites (such as other blogging services, wikis, or your own school server) would follow similar procedures right up until the point of uploading.

Adapted from a document originally developed by Paul Allison and numerous collaborators, available online at docs.google.com/Doc?docid=ah5m9qjtkbwf_27mcjg27&hl=en.

(Courtesy of Paul Allison; used with permission.)

FIGURE 6.4

How to create a basic podcast

Recording a Basic Podcast

- Be sure that your microphone is plugged in and selected as your audio input device (Windows: Control Panel -> Sounds and Audio Devices; Mac: System Preferences: Sound -> Input)
- Begin recording your podcast by hitting the red "record" button in Audacity. When finished, push the yellow "Stop" button.
- If you choose to do any editing, note the six tool buttons in the upper left-hand corner of the program. With them, you can perform the following tasks:
  - To edit out portions of the recording, choose the "Selection Tool" and then highlight the portion of your timeline that you want to delete. Once highlighted, hit the "delete" button to remove that section.
  - If you want to record multiple tracks for your podcast, or insert music, and blend the tracks together, use the "Time Shift Tool," to arrange different layers of tracks.
  - If you want to change the volume of any part of your tracks, including fade ins and outs, use the "Envelope Tool." Select the point on your timeline that you want the fade to begin and click to put a marker in. Then, select where you want the fade to end and you will notice that the amplitude of the timeline can be reduced, thus decreasing the volume of the track.
- Periodically, save your project in a convenient folder on your computer. Audacity creates .aup files in which all the associated materials from a project are stored.

Exporting and Formatting a Basic Podcast

Once your podcast is complete, you can condense it into an MP3 file. The first time that Audacity creates an MP3, you will have to associate the LAME MP3 encoder during the saving process. This happens only once, and you will be linking to the LAME file that you saved previously.

- Choose "File" and "Export as MP3"
- For the first run, follow the directions to associate the LAME MP3 encoder.
- Choose a name and location for the file to be saved.
- Complete the ID3 tags with artist, title, album, and genre information. These can be changed later using iTunes.
- Export the MP3
- Open iTunes, choose "File" and then "Add to Library"
- Navigate to the MP3 file you just saved and click "Open."
- Once imported into iTunes, right click (Windows) or Command-click (Mac) on the name of the track
- Choose "Get Info" and then select the "Info" tab
- Make sure that the artist, title, album, and genre information are correct
- Click "OK" to save any changes

For further information on how to post your podcast see digitalwritingworkshop.ning.com

Looking Ahead: Imagining a Framework for Instruction in Your Digital Writing Workshop

No question, assessment is complicated, as is the process of digital writing. Unlike other "Looking Ahead" sections of this book, where I offer a particular technology tool for thinking about how to use digital writing, the best suggestion that I can offer here is that you ask your students to document their work over time in a variety of ways and, ideally, in a centralized location such as a class wiki where they can embed media or link to other work they have online. For instance, taking screenshots of two versions of a document and writing a reflection on the changes would be one way to share their thinking. Trying to imagine new ways to assess digital writing while the tools and practices keep shifting under our feet is, at best, difficult. Educators and researchers have spent nearly three decades articulating the six traits assessment, for instance, and while it often produces reliable results, it still has drawbacks. Thus, thinking about how to assess digital writing will raise even more questions about reliability and will also have flaws.

Also, as noted in the opening chapter of this book and reiterated throughout, there is a tension that comes from learning about and working with new literacies, both because they are different than what we are accustomed to and because we are asking students to engage in practices that they use outside of school within the confines of school. The process of multimedia composing can become, unfortunately, rather artificial once we try to make it more "academic" requiring certain steps and outcomes.

Any proposal for a pedagogy of teaching digital writing, indeed for structuring a digital writing workshop, must account for the formative and the summative, the process and the product, not to mention both the tools and the techniques. It is with this idea in mind that I developed the framework in Chapter 7 for creating your digital writing workshop, which I hope will guide your instruction by looking at the students you teach, the subject of digital writing itself, and the spaces in which digital writing occurs, both physical and virtual.

Creating Your Digital Writing Workshop

Throughout this book, we have explored the ways in which digital writing tools can be employed to meet the goals of our writing workshop. By building on the writing workshop principles of inquiry and choice (Chapter 2), conferring and response (Chapter 3), examining author's craft (Chapter 4), publishing beyond the classroom (Chapter 5), and broadening our visions of assessment (Chapter 6), digital writing tools can sometimes supplement, sometimes enhance, and sometimes completely change the ways in which we work with writers. Digital writing changes a number of dynamics in the writing process, and there are implications for three of those dynamics that seem to be most pronounced: the *students* we teach, the *subject* matter of writing, and the *spaces* in which writing occurs. By offering some guiding questions and action steps for each of these three dynamics—students, subject matter, and spaces—my intent is for you to be able to create your digital writing workshop based not on inflexible steps, but on a dynamic and fluid model that acknowledges the context in which you teach.

First, a brief aside to clarify my perspective. After having spent a number of years as a teacher who both participated in and then led technology-related professional development, including a laptops-for-teachers initiative in the state of Michigan, a virtual high school instructor training program, the National Writing Project's Technology Matters Advanced Institutes and National Technology Initiative, and a yearlong technology and literacy experience called Project WRITE (Writing, Reading, Inquiry, and Technology Education) through the Red Cedar Writing Project, I have come to the realization in my own teaching and work with teachers that technology is not neutral, nor can a particular technology be applied the same way across all classrooms. That is, any particular technology—such as a word processor, slide show program, or wiki—can be employed for a variety of purposes, some of which engage students in productive digital writing practices and some of which simply replicate what we have always done with pencil and paper. Thus, teachers need to understand how and why to employ technology in specific ways. I agree with Punya Mishra and Matthew Koehler, who describe a concept of "technological pedagogical content knowledge" (now referred to as TPACK; for more information, visit tpack.org/) that suggests there is

> no single technological solution that applies for every teacher, every course, or every view of teaching. Quality teaching requires developing a nuanced understanding of the complex relationships between technology, content, and pedagogy, and using this understanding to develop appropriate, context-specific strategies and representations. (2006, 1029)

As I have been arguing throughout this book, context matters, which is the reason for structuring the book around key principles in the writing workshop first and technologies second. We should each create a digital writing workshop based on a number of factors, namely our students, our conception of the subject we call writing, and the spaces, both physical and virtual, in which we teach. In order to do this, we might first think about how our conceptions of writing, and teaching writing, have changed in the past few decades and then consider some questions and action steps for adapting these beliefs to digital writing.

How Did We Get Here? Where Are We Going?

From the beginning of the process writing movement, teachers have been trying to invite student writers to see audiences and purposes beyond the classroom and traditional school genres. Going through a process, rather than just focusing on a final product, helped students understand that writing does not just pop out of the pencil or get tapped on a keyboard in a perfect state. But, even when the writing process approach took hold, I always felt that there was still something a bit insincere about this writing. Yes, it was shared with peers in class. Yes, it was read at the author's chair or published in a school anthology. Yes, it went home and made it on the fridge. And, if it was lucky, that student writing made it to a local newspaper or other venue for publication. But school-based writing was—for all intents—distributed to limited audiences, even if it was written for a variety of purposes.

The read/write web finally delivered the promise of having a real audience and varied purposes that writing teachers had so long looked to bring to their classrooms. Suddenly, writing teachers felt as if their students could have a purpose and audience beyond the classroom and school. Some were able to publish their writing online in the early days of the Internet, but technical problems got in the way, such as not knowing how to edit HTML or upload files to a server. The promise of the Web was to democratize information—and it did, if you could figure out how to create web pages and upload them. So, when read/write web tools such as blogs and wikis emerged, and push-button publishing became possible for anyone, anywhere, the goal of "publishing" work for an authentic audience and purpose finally emerged as a goal for writers, both in and out of school. We could write (and publish our writing) anytime, anywhere. In an increasingly networked world, writers need to adapt to different purposes, audiences, and contexts for writing that have been enabled by newer technologies. This also involves a shift in how we think about who writers are, how texts are produced, and where texts are distributed.

Yet just because we have access to the tools does not mean that students are engaged in digital writing. Regardless of how digital we think our students are—and, no doubt, as many reports in the news media and research studies such as Tapscott (2008) and the Pew Internet and American Life Project (Lenhart et al. 2008) confirm, most of them are more adept than their elders at particular digital skills like texting, blogging, uploading photos or videos, and using social networks such as Facebook—they do not necessarily possess the capacities that make them critical and creative digital writers. Not only do they need to understand the technical aspects of creating hyperlinks, posting to a blog, or collaborating with a wiki, but they need to have the intentional focus as a writer to understand the audience and purpose for which they are writing. Moreover, they need to consider the ways in which we can compose with multiple modes and media. As Warschauer (2006) argues, a combination of new mind-sets for teachers, administrators, students, parents, and other stakeholders must accompany substantive change in literacy practices enabled by technology. Understanding when, why, and how to use different forms of media to convey a particular message requires a working knowledge of the mode—that is, what an audience expects from a piece of writing in order to be moved to action—and how to effectively manipulate the media in which it is composed.

In short, students must be made aware of the ways in which their writing is distributed and perceived across the many networks in which they participate, in school and out. And writing teachers need to consider the many ways in which students see themselves as writers (and sometimes fail to see themselves as writers, according to a Pew report by Lenhart et al. 2008) and invite them to be intentional about how they read and write in a digital age.

Thus, writing has always been a complex act, and relying on our long history of understanding the writing process as well as the writing workshop approach helps us now understand how newer technologies can offer writers numerous opportunities to get their message across. Writing in a digital world means that, as writers and teachers of writing, we need to be aware of these choices and how we can best utilize them to have the intended effect on our various audiences. We need to understand the ways in which writing has been taught in order to better understand our students, the subject matter of writing, and the spaces in which digital writing happens.

Exploring the Dynamics of the Digital Writing Workshop: Students, Subject, and Spaces

In considering the ways in which we can design our digital writing workshops, and building on the principles of the writing workshop as identified in this book, it helps me to have a pedagogical framework through which I can make decisions about how I teach. In that sense, I find it important to ask questions and take action steps that help me better understand my students as digital writers, the subject of digital writing, and the spaces, real and virtual, in which digital writing is taught.

Return once again to the image of Aram Kabodian's students, presented in Chapter 1, and consider the students who are composing their public service announcements (PSAs) as digital videos using a mobile laptop lab. What would be different, for instance, in this digital writing workshop if the students were located in a computer lab with desktop computers, using a different form of media to create their PSAs, such as a website or slide show presentation? When we consider the ways that students can work, individually and collaboratively, the actual tasks facing them as digital writers, and the tools that they are able to work with, the teaching context changes (DeVoss, Cushman, and Grabill

2005). In turn, the ways in which you structure your digital writing workshop will change, too, based on your students, the actual elements of digital writing you study, and the spaces in which you work.

To that end, as you craft your digital writing workshop, I offer you the following critical questions and action steps so that you can begin to think through the many possibilities for digital writing tools in your classroom and how to employ them in support of student writers.

Students: Who Are the Digital Writers We Teach?

As we consider the students with whom we work each day, we can easily fall into a pattern of stereotyping that positions them in different, sometimes unflattering ways. For instance, we may see them as digital natives, yet they may not have the skills and abilities to create and critique all the kinds of digital media that they consume. We may also see them in the trappings of adolescence, acting in their own self-interest and without regard for consequences. Yet doing either of these things suggests that we neither see each student as an individual nor see that each is capable of making decisions about the ways in which she employs digital writing tools for purposes in and out of school. We need to enable our students to be conscientious collaborators, in all senses of the term. They need to be able to work together to create digital writing as well as be able to respond effectively to the digital writing of others. In order to meet this goal, we need to rely on the technical expertise and interpersonal skills that they have and guide them in ways that help them learn about digital writing.

Critical Questions to Consider for Students in Your Digital Writing Workshop

- Overall, in what ways do you view your students and their uses of technology—positively, negatively, or neutrally? Do you see them as capable, naïve, or more advanced than yourself?
- Are there specific technologies such as social networking, text messaging, blogs, wikis, or other web-enabled applications that your students claim to use on a regular basis? What are these technologies, and in what ways do you understand and use them yourself, if at all? In what ways could they productively be used to support digital writing instruction?
- How do your students view digital writing? That is, do they call instant messaging, text messaging, and blogging "writing"? In what ways do

they see digital writing as enhanced by, or at least a part of, school-based writing?

- Outside of school, how often do your students have access to Internet-enabled computers for sustained periods of time? In those contexts, how many have a trusted adult to whom they can turn if a problem—technical or ethical—pops up?

- In what ways do students understand their rights as producers and distributors of digital texts? To what extent do they critically think about fair use as well as how to employ copyright-free or copyright-friendly materials as appropriate?

Action Steps to Take with Students

- Ask a student whom you trust and who trusts you to take you on a tour of his profile on a social networking site (of course, this may require leaving school to get to an Internet connection that is not filtered). While surfing the site with him, ask about the ways in which he composes a public persona using text, images, audio, and video.

- If you have not yet already done so, create a blog or a wiki using the digital writing tools discussed in this book and invite students to contribute content to the site. I promise, you cannot break them, so take time to play around with the different settings; you can always change them back. I also promise that if students post inappropriate material, you can take it down. If possible, work with a colleague in this process to discuss how, why, and when you might employ this tool in your classroom.

- If you are not ready to take the plunge with an entire class, invite a small group of trusted students to create a project with one of the digital writing tools described in this text. During that process, ask them to record the different tasks that go into composing a piece of digital writing. Once done, review the piece as well as the list of tasks with them to discuss what they learned about the writing process as well as the digital writing tools.

Subject: What Do We Teach When We Teach Digital Writing?

As noted throughout this book and simply summarized here, digital writing changes the contexts and purposes for writing. The study of the subject of writing—including the elements of craft, the study of genres, and the many ways in which writing can be created and distributed through different media—has become even more critical in an age of newer technologies. Thus, a definition of writing as simply putting words on paper (or screen) is not sufficient in this age, and we need to carefully consider what it means to be a writer and a teacher of writing in relation to digital texts. As the subject matter of writing continues to evolve, however, we can ask fundamental questions about what it means to write and be a writer, and these questions can guide us as we create our digital writing workshops.

Critical Questions to Consider About the Content of Writing in Your Digital Writing Workshop

- In your experience as a writer, what counts as writing? How does writing with a computer change or challenge your notion of what a text is? What does it mean to be a writer in a digital age?
- As a reader of digital texts—web pages, videos, audio, images—what qualities do you most appreciate? What elements of craft do you try to emulate in your own digital reading (such as bookmarking, tagging, annotating, and sharing) and writing (such as using multimedia and hyperlinks)?
- To what extent do you understand provisions of fair use in copyright law and your rights to create transformative uses of copyrighted work through digital writing? To what extent do you understand the idea of copyright-friendly work, such as items licensed through Creative Commons, and the ways in which these items can be used in digital writing?
- What elements of genre or principles of good writing are common across all texts, print and digital? In what ways can we transfer our understandings of good print-based writing into ideas about what constitutes good digital writing?
- Curriculum guidelines and standardized assessments offer us particular visions of what counts as writing. In what ways does digital writing replicate or resist these visions? What implications does that have for how we approach the task of teaching writing?
- What does the writing process look like with digital writing?

Action Steps to Take for the Subject of Digital Writing

- Craft a variety of modes using one digital writing tool. For instance, in separate blog posts, write a piece of fiction, a piece of nonfiction, and a personal reflection. If you are utilizing the tools available related to the particular medium, add digital writing elements. In the case of a blog post, for instance, embed images, create hyperlinks, and experiment with fonts. Discuss with a colleague the ways in which your writing process changes, both across modes and across media such as podcasts, digital stories, and wikis.

- Look for examples of good digital writing and discuss with a colleague what makes the writing strong. What elements of author's craft are present? What does the piece do, digitally, that it could not do as well, or do at all, as a print-based piece?
- Reflect on the process of guiding your students through a piece of digital writing. In what ways are the minilessons that you created similar to and different from the typical types of lessons that you develop?

Spaces: When, Where, and How Do We Teach Digital Writing?

We teach digital writing in both face-to-face as well as virtual spaces. During a single class period, some of our students may interact with each other more by simply talking to one another, while some may interact entirely online. The ways in which we set up our classrooms, both literally and figuratively, matter a great deal to the success of individual writers as well as the overall feeling within the writing community. As we create conditions for a successful digital writing workshop, we need to think carefully about the ways in which we structure the spaces to meet our pedagogical goals and support students in their individual writing practices.

Questions About the Spaces in Which You Teach in Your Digital Writing Workshop

- Questions about physical space:
  - Are the computers set up in a manner that is ergonomically sound as well as flexible enough for students to see others in the room over the screens?
  - If you are working with fixed desktop computers, are there any flexible spaces in the room where students can easily collaborate, either around one computer or in a small group away from the computers? If you are working with laptops, can students easily move furniture to gather around a single computer or in small groups?
  - To what extent are students able to move from machine to machine in order to help one another when questions arise?

- Questions about virtual spaces:
  - What digital writing tool is best suited for the task at hand (for instance, using a blog to record a chronological travelogue as compared with using a wiki to create an interactive tourist guidebook)?
  - How are students invited in, implicitly and explicitly, to be a part of the space? Do they need user names and passwords? To what extent do you discuss the norms of the space and create opportunities for students to learn those norms and help maintain the community?
  - How do you help students create good responses to one another's texts so that writers feel both honored to have shared their work and as if they are getting substantive feedback, knowing that the feedback will be made public?
  - Will you have a centralized space (such as a class wiki), or will you allow students to post their work using whatever service they choose? What are the advantages and disadvantages to both methods?

Action Steps to Take for Space

- Creating physical spaces:
  - Depending on the space in which you generally teach your digital writing workshop and its limitations in terms of furniture, desktops versus laptops, and use by other teachers, attempt to create as open a classroom as possible. Having small pods of computers or tables along the outside walls where computers sit allows for easy movement and communication. Also, like a traditional writing workshop, having the tools that writers need easily available around the room (such as pens, pencils, paper, dictionaries, and other items) will allow for students to take breaks from their computer screens and write or draw.
- Creating virtual spaces:
  - Depending on the digital writing tool that you choose, you will have more or less control over how students access your virtual classroom space and what changes you can see that they have made to it. A wiki, for instance, will track everything that a user does, from page edits to discussion posts, if they are logged in. A blog shows who wrote and approved posts for public view. Putting a digital story on a video-sharing site or a photo-essay on a photo-sharing site requires a user name and login.
  - Create a central space for your digital writing workshop, most likely a blog or a wiki. Keeping track of the students' work becomes a bigger

logistical concern as they employ different spaces, so having them post their work to a centralized location becomes critical. Explore the samples of blogs and wikis noted throughout the book to see how different teachers are creating spaces for their students to post and respond to others' work.

Conclusion

With all the ideas I've discussed about the digital writing workshop, let me reiterate my caveat that technology is not an add-on or bag of tricks for writing teachers for the twenty-first century; instead technology and writing must be seen as intricately intertwined. For example, the pedagogical choices that you make when you set up a blog—such as creating individual blogs or having all students post to a class blog—affects what you can or cannot do with your students. Understanding the affordances and constraints of different digital writing tools, as well as your own goals for why you are employing those tools, highlights the ways in which Mishra and Koehler's TPACK framework as well as the questions outlined in this chapter can help you structure your digital writing workshop.

As you create your digital writing workshop, you will inevitably be faced with technology hurdles and questions about what you expect students to actually do with their compositions. My hope is that you can explore these ideas with your own students and colleagues, as well as with the community of teachers who also want to learn about how to create a digital writing workshop on our social network: digitalwritingworkshop.ning.com/.

From my experience as a digital writer, and as a teacher of digital writing, I encourage you to take the risk of engaging in this type of writing with your students. While it might challenge your notions of what you should know and be able to do as a teacher, invite your students into the process and, most importantly, don't worry because learning is a collaborative experience. You're not expected to know all the answers; you're just expected to support their growth as writers and readers in an ever-evolving digital age.

Making those connections is what teaching in a digital writing workshop is all about. Enjoy the journey.

Appendix 1
Sample Lessons: Exploring Copyright Through Collaborative Wiki Writing

Global economies, new technologies, and exponential growth in information are transforming our society. Today's employees engage with a technology-driven, diverse, and quickly changing "flat world." English/ language arts teachers need to prepare students for this world with problem solving, collaboration, and analysis—as well as skills with word processing, hyper-text, LCDs, Web cams, digital streaming podcasts, smartboards, and social networking software—central to individual and community success.

—National Council of Teachers of English,
21st-Century Literacies: A Policy Research Brief

As we prepare students to be literate in the twenty-first century, NCTE and other professional organizations encourage us to teach them how to manage their digital lives in personally, professionally, and academically responsible ways. Copyright law, a key component of literacy in an increasingly digital culture, guides us all as we strive to understand the rights that we have as consumers of others' work, as well as the rights that we have as producers of our own work. By engaging students in a problem-based model of learning and collaborative writing—with a wiki at the center of their communication—

Originally published in a slightly different form in *Classroom Notes Plus* 26, no. 2 (NCTE 2008): 7–15. Reprinted by permission.

this series of lessons for middle and high school students explores how copyright functions and invites students to learn how to utilize digital materials appropriately.

At the center of this series of lessons, you will rely on a web-based tool called a wiki: a web page that can be collaboratively composed, edited, and commented upon by multiple contributors. By working through the scenarios related to copyright and inviting students to collaborate digitally with a wiki, we can introduce them to the power that comes from building off the ideas of others and remixing them with their own. Thus, they can be effective twenty-first-century collaborators while still respecting copyright and the ethics of intellectual property. This series of lessons is estimated to require about a week to two weeks, assuming five to seven class sessions with computer access, plus two to four additional hours outside class during which students are researching and writing online, whether in the computer lab, at home, or at the library.

A few logistical notes. First, these lessons will require students to have regular Internet access at school and, ideally, at home. The digital divide remains a real problem in many of our schools and communities, but teachers whose students do not have home access to the Internet should still be able to accomplish these lessons with some additional planning. Assuming that students have access to computers in the classroom, in the school computer lab, or at the local library, teachers can spread the activities out over time, so that students have more in-school time to work as well as more time to arrange library visits and other options.

Second, you might be wondering what a wiki is, let alone how to use one. Teachers from around the world have created many online guides, tutorials, and videos to help you get started with using wikis. An hour or two of browsing the sites listed here and viewing examples of other education wikis will be enough to familiarize you with the basics of this simple-to-use tool. Then you'll be ready to start your own, which for a free wiki usually involves little more than providing your name and email, naming your new wiki page, and typing an introduction to your first page.

To get started, first review Mark Wagner's presentation from the K–12 Online Conference in 2006, "Wiki While You Work (Basic)" (k12online conference.org/?p=53), which offers his presentation and links to many other wiki resources. After that, try out a few wiki sites. The wiki site that I prefer is Wikispaces (www.wikispaces.com/), as it offers ad-free spaces for teachers, but you could use any of a variety of sites, such as PBworks (pbworks.com/) or Wetpaint (www.wetpaint.com/). By getting a sense of the different interfaces and what the wikis look like to you as a viewer and editor, you will have a better sense of how to help your students use your wiki.

On the surface, a wiki looks like most other web pages with text, images, and links (see Figure A.1). When you move into editing mode, they offer a word-processor-style "what you see is what you get" (WYSIWYG) function, allowing you to add text and embed media such as videos and pictures (see Figure A.2). Moreover, wikis have discussion and history pages, which allow for users to add comments and also review versions of the page, respectively. Once you are familiar with these functions, you will be able to describe them to students, too, who will also quickly figure out how to use them. While I know it is very nerve-racking for us all, as teachers, to talk to our students about things that we ourselves are not quite sure about, I can assure you that every time I have introduced wikis to students, they have caught on very quickly, often helping me understand something new in the process. Trust that they will help you, too.

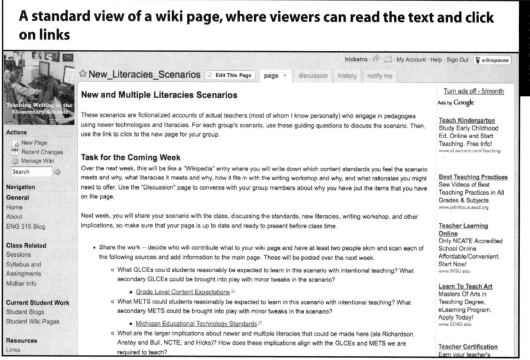

A standard view of a wiki page, where viewers can read the text and click on links

FIGURE A.1

An editor's view of a wiki page. Notice the WYSIWYG editing bar across the top and that the text is editable, much like a word-processing document.

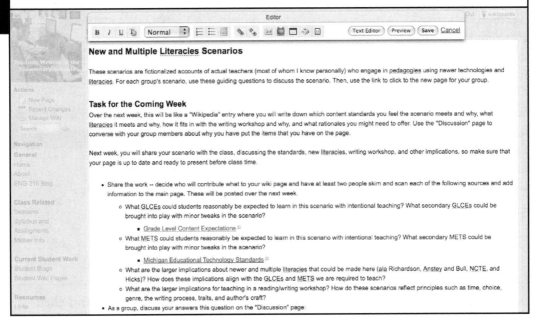

Complicating Copyright in a Digital Age

Digital media—as the multiple lawsuits and congressional hearings about file-sharing services like Napster attest—have malleable properties that allow content to be in different places all at once, unlike traditional print texts, images, and art. The ways in which we use digital media—from PDFs to MP3s to JPEGs—have less to do with where we got the file from (and whether or not we purchased the rights to use it) than they have to do with where the file is legally and ethically permitted to be used or shared. In short, thinking about copyright and intellectual property has become a part of how we communicate through text, image, and sound, and, in turn, has become a topic critical to English language arts instruction.

Why is it critical? First, if we want to teach our students good research and citation practices, then we need to model them.

Part of that process is understanding fair use and the rights and responsibilities that teachers and students have when using copyrighted work. Fair use relies on four tests to determine whether copyright has been infringed: the purpose of use, the nature of the copyrighted work, the amount of work used, and the effect of the use on the work's market (en.wikipedia.org/wiki/Fair_use). It is worth brushing up on these principles. Hall Davidson has created a chart that explains fair use for teachers, and it is worth taking a look at to see if the materials that you are using in your classroom fall under fair-use guidelines (www.halldavidson.net/copyright_chart.pdf). We as teachers are sometimes guilty of telling our students to cite the intellectual property of others while we violate copyright laws, a double standard that we cannot continue to hold. Also worth viewing is Eric Faden's *A Fair(y) Use Tale*, which uses short clips of Disney movies to illustrate the four principles of educational fair use (www.youtube.com/watch?v=CJn_jC4FNDo).[1]

Second, there is a new ethos emerging about how and why to use digital media, including text, images, videos, and sounds.

While there are many items that students and teachers can use that are in the public domain (see, for instance, the Library of Congress at www.loc.gov/ and kitZu at kitzu.org/ for a number of items that are available for use in the public domain), there are many things that we cannot. Think of the story of people who got sued for putting Mickey Mouse images on their websites. Stanford law professor Lawrence Lessig (www.lessig.org/) and a number of others have generated a new idea about how we can share our ideas through digital media, because it is different than other media we are used to such as books and tapes. With the advent of the Internet and the sharing of digital media, we are now able to download, remix, and upload digital content. Lessig and others have developed a new form of copyright, Creative Commons (creativecommons.org/), that allows content creators to retain certain rights to their work while permitting others to use it as well in their own creations. There are movies and comics on the site that outline how Creative Commons functions, thus describing the different ways in which creators can allow for different uses of their work. For another succinct explanation of Creative Commons, view Educause's "7 Things You Should Know About Creative Commons" handout (educause.edu/ELI/7 ThingsYouShouldKnowAboutCreat/156826).

---

1. As noted in first chapter of this book, my thinking on copyright and fair use has continued to evolve over the past few years, especially given the recent publication of the *Code of Best Practices in Fair Use for Media Literacy Education* (Center for Social Media 2008), available at mediaeducation lab.com/sites/mediaeducationlab.com/files/CodeofBestPracticesinFairUse.pdf.

The Creative Commons website also allows you to search and find images (on flickr.com/), video (on blip.tv/), music (on www.owlmm.com/), and sound clips (on www.freesound.org/). The Creative Commons site has movies and comics that explain all the history and uses of their licenses—resources that could be explored as part of this lesson or in a follow-up assignment.

Understanding copyright law (along with fair use and Creative Commons) has become a key component of being a reader and writer in our digital age, and lessons related to copyright, intellectual property, and digital media will help your students understand the many ways in which they can integrate the ideas of others into their own work, both creatively and ethically.

Step 1: Inviting Students to Think About Wikis (One Class Period)

Our students have been called the Net Generation, the Millenials, digital natives, and a number of other names that capture the spirit of the times: bits and bytes, gadgets and gizmos, shorter attention spans and faster forms of communication. While I agree with many of these descriptions, I also agree with the many teachers and scholars that contend students may be able to operate these gadgets, but they may not be utilizing them in critical and creative ways to read and write about their world. So, at the same time I suggest we try to appeal to digital learners through multimodal communication, I also suggest that we add the value that we can, as adults and educators, in helping them think carefully about the decisions that they make when they choose and then use these tools.

For this first lesson, begin with a journal prompt or class discussion, asking students what they know about wikis. One place to begin this conversation is by asking students about Wikipedia as well as discussing your own stance on this open-source encyclopedia. You could ask them what they know about how Wikipedia entries are produced, how often they are changed, and why some teachers (perhaps even your entire school) do not want students using Wikipedia as a source. Capture their initial ideas on a whiteboard or, perhaps, by typing them up on your wiki as a new page.

Next, to provide a better sense of how wikis work, show students the *Common Craft Show*'s video "Wikis in Plain English" (www.commoncraft.com/

video-wikis-plain-english). This four-minute video gives a simple, clear introduction to wikis, using the example of a group of people who use a wiki to plan a camping trip. After showing the video, see if students can think of other situations in which a wiki could be useful. Typical ideas might include planning a party, writing song lyrics, planning a family vacation, creating a memory book of stories for a family member, and so on. Remind them that they will be creating a wiki page themselves soon and to think about the issues that they will have to deal with as individual and collaborative authors.

Another helpful link to share with students is National Public Radio's *On the Media* report "Get Me Rewrite," an eight-minute interview with author and instructor Clay Shirky about Wikipedia, how it was developed, how the Wikipedia community handles problems such as bad information and vandalism, and questions of "expertise and authoritativeness" (www.onthemedia.org/transcripts/transcripts_070805_rewrite.html).

To help students absorb the ideas as they listen, you may want to print out the online transcript and make it available to students to write on while you play the audio clip.

If time allows, engage students in follow-up discussion with questions like the following:

- What are the risks of using an online reference like Wikipedia, which can be edited at any time by any of the users?
- What are the benefits of using an online reference like Wikipedia, especially in terms of timeliness of the information?
- If you needed to find reliable information on an important topic, would you trust Wikipedia as a source? Justify your answer as to why you would or would not.
- What does Clay Shirky mean when he says, "What makes a wiki good is not the technology, but the community"? How does this idea relate to the wiki page that you and your peers are going to build?

Listening to and discussing these two segments will help familiarize students with wikis and will also prompt them to engage in deeper thinking and discussion about collaboration, authority, and how knowledge is made in our culture. At the end of this lesson, invite students to weigh the pros and cons of working on a wiki, as both a reader and a writer (see Figure A.3). There are many ways in which students might think about these pros and cons (see Figure A.4).

Wiki pros and cons matrix

After viewing "Wikis in Plain English" and listening to "Get Me Rewrite," work with a partner to discuss the pros and cons of reading and writing wikis. Think about this from a technical aspect, as well as from the perspective of being a collaborative author.

	Advantages to You as a Writer/Reader	Disadvantages to You as a Writer/Author
Online access to the wiki and interface		
Ability to edit other's work (and potentially overwrite it at the same time)		
Ability to comment on the discussion page		
Ability to see the history of revisions		
Ability to add multimedia such as hyperlinks, sounds, and videos		
Ability to create additional pages		
Ability to evaluate authoritativeness of content		
Other:		

Sample wiki pros and cons matrix

After viewing "Wikis in Plain English" and listening to "Get Me Rewrite," work with a partner to discuss the pros and cons of reading and writing wikis. Think about this from a technical aspect, as well as from the perspective of being a collaborative author.

	Advantages to You as a Writer/Reader	Disadvantages to You as a Writer/Author
Online access to the wiki and interface	• Can get to it at home, school, or the library • Don't need to save a file on a jump drive	• Can forget your login • Others could be editing the page
Ability to edit other's work (and potentially overwrite it at the same time)	• Can help edit your collaborators' work while at home or school, working alone or together	• Can reverse changes that others have made • Your changes are tracked, so people can see if you have made a mistake, too
Ability to comment on the discussion page	• Can carry on discussions about group's wiki page • Can post questions to teacher or other peers	• May not be used effectively • People may not check the discussion page
Ability to see the history of revisions	• Helps show growth of article • Can see individual contributions	• All changes are tracked, including errors • Page can be reverted accidentally
Ability to add multimedia such as hyperlinks, sounds, and videos	• Can create a richer text with multimedia • Could incorporate copyright-friendly materials as examples	• Page can become overloaded with multimedia, losing focus • Copyrighted materials may be included inadvertently
Ability to create additional pages	• Groups can supplement ideas on their "home" page, including definitions or examples	• Adding additional links could become confusing or detract from the central content
Ability to evaluate authoritativeness of content	• Since the work is produced by students, it will appeal to their sensibilities of audience	• Mechanical errors in the writing as well as factual errors in the content could confuse the reader
Other:		

Step 2: Inviting Students to Work with Wikis (One Class Period)

Begin by reviewing students' pros and cons chart from day one. After students have a conceptual understanding of wikis, it is time to have them do some nuts-and-bolts work. When I set up wikis for my classes, the first thing that I do is have students each create their own page, so they can practice working on the wiki without overwriting each other. To do this, I ask them to create a new page on our wiki, using their name as the title. Then, I create one page with all of their names in a bulleted list so they can go back to that master list and insert a hyperlink to their own page. You could include your own name in the list, too, so as to show students how to highlight it and make a new link in the editing mode, thus creating your own page. Sometimes, early in the process, I intentionally ask a few students to edit this page at the same time so they can see how writing over others' edits could be potentially devastating if a group hasn't saved its work in a while. It is a good warning, so they do not actually lose a lot of work later on. If time allows, it would be good to have students post pictures to their wiki page, make links to other sites that they are interested in, and add some text about themselves, all to get used to the wiki interface. Of course, there is always the caveat about privacy here, so remind students not to post anything that is in any way personal or private, or that they do not have permission to post.

From my experiences working with students and teachers who are learning new technologies, I find that giving people time to play and explore is helpful, and that is what I encourage you to do for at least thirty minutes of this class period. While it may seem like this is a great deal of unstructured time, you can invite students who have mastered these basics to help those who have not. By the end of the period, everyone should have his own page on the wiki as an example, and allowing students to help one another will ensure they all reach that goal.

Once students have a basic understanding of the wiki interface, it is time to introduce them to the idea of creating a page on their wiki with a group. Discuss how the main page should reflect the consensus of the group, and point out that they can use the discussion page to hammer out disagreements or have more extended discussions about how to present their work. By stipulating that the main wiki page should present a unified voice, you are encouraging students to work collaboratively and helping them understand how the act of coming to consensus becomes a part of their writing process. Potential jumping-off points for class discussion at this stage include:

- how to find a group focus for their writing while maintaining individual responsibility to contribute;
- understanding when and how to edit others' writing, as well as the differences between editing and revision; and
- how to deal with personality conflicts, both online and offline.

You can end the class period with a discussion of these ideas, as working together will continue to be a theme of the groups' work throughout the rest of the unit.

Step 3: Introducing Scenarios for Student Groups (One Class Period)

Now that students have an understanding of the wiki interface and the beginning of a group page, you can set up scenarios, which students will discuss, research, and ultimately base their wiki pages on. You will want to share some of the information about fair use and Creative Commons. I encourage you to explore these resources and construct this particular lesson in a way that fits both the time you have available as well as what you think your students will be able to understand about fair use and Creative Commons.

Depending on the age level you are working with, you might tweak these examples a bit, but I generally find that giving students an authentic problem engages them in the process. For instance, rather than ask them, "Is it ethical to download music from the Internet?" you might set up a more nuanced scenario like this:

> You and your friends have formed a band and want to distribute your music online. Some of the songs you play are covers, while some are original with your own lyrics. What are the legal implications of sharing your music and how would you go about deciding how to do so? What copyright protections, if any, would you put on your own original music?

While each scenario may not relate to the typical topics of English class such as writing essays and reading literature in an apples-to-apples way, the idea behind creating scenarios is to get students discussing the many issues related to copyright and, by extension, the types of twenty-first-century literacies key to finding and using materials in an appropriate manner. You can develop simple scenarios to address a variety of other topics related to production and consumption of digital texts, such as these:

- Downloading and remixing music through legal means such as iTunes, illegal means such as BitTorrent, or copyright-free means such as the royalty-free Freeplay Music or other Creative Commons sites. Also, the implications of digital rights management (DRM) and file type, where certain files can be played only on certain media players.
- Recording and posting videos of copyright-protected video broadcasts, from sitcoms to sports to the evening news on sites such as YouTube. Similar questions about DRM are applicable here, too.
- Remixing materials from Creative Commons sites to create new media such as podcasts, digital stories, or music, and making proper citation and attribution credits. Moreover, deciding what kind of license to put on your own work.
- Downloading a text from Project Gutenberg (www.gutenberg.org/) and copying and pasting sections of that text into a new text. For instance, creating character blogs or profiles from *Macbeth* that incorporate significant chunks of Shakespeare's text, copied and pasted directly from Project Gutenberg.

You can develop additional scenarios based on your own curriculum, school context, and interests, or potentially from students' own experiences working with materials from the Internet. For all of these topics and scenarios, ask students to explore the copyright implications when using the text outright or using parts for interpretation or critical analysis.

Also, invite students to discuss the implications of rebroadcasting the text online, or only within your classroom, and how that changes the ways that they can use the text. In all scenarios, students should explore the terms of use or copyright agreement and make explicit reference to what the content owners will allow, what fair-use policy dictates, and their own ethical judgment.

Next students build the case for what they will argue on their scenario homepage. They must justify why and how they should, could, or would use particular content and what fair-use provision they would apply in order to use it.

They must also find cases that are similar to their own, offering interpretation of how each case was decided and, if appropriate, links to other web resources that could contribute to their overall argument. Each scenario will largely be composed as a collaborative text, yet it could take on multimodal components, too, through the addition of links, photos, video clips, and so on. They should wrap up this initial discussion during class time, as they will all begin to contribute to the wiki page inside and outside of class over the next few days.

Step 4: Teaching Collaboration and Coauthorship (Two to Three Class Periods, with Homework)

Teaching students how to work together, let alone write together, remains one of the most challenging tasks in teaching writing. Part of our task as teachers, then, is to help students see the many ways in which they can collaborate and encourage them to move toward a coauthored form of writing where they are engaging in their individual writing, peer editing and revision, and crafting a unified voice in their final piece.

In *Writing Together: Collaborative Learning in the Writing Classroom*, Tori Haring-Smith (1994) suggests that collaborative writing can take many forms, from the traditional peer response and editing and brainstorming or planning that a group might do all the way through writing with one another. Once students move beyond these phases of talk and support for each other's writing, she defines the act of collaborative writing in three potential manners:

- *Serial writing*: In this mode of collaborative writing, a "train of individuals" works on a text. This could take the form of employees creating individual sections to a report that the supervisor compiles and sends out without further collaboration. This would be cooperation at its basic level. (361–62)
- *Compiled writing*: Here, individuals all add components of the text and retain "some control over part of the final text" so the reader can tell who wrote what. This might be a collection of essays or poems. This would be a more advanced form of cooperation, because all the parts have to fit, but there is not a great deal of negotiation among all the writers that goes into this kind of writing. (362–63)
- *Coauthored writing*: In this type of writing, "it is difficult (indeed, often impossible) to distinguish the work of one writer from another." In terms

of collaboration, this would be a text where all authors have a stake in what is said. There is often one facilitator here who coordinates the final draft of the text, but everyone is expected to contribute equally in terms of the content, revision, and editing. (363–65)

Before, during, and after students work in their groups over the course of a few class periods, discuss each of these kinds of collaborative writing and ask students to evaluate and jot notes about where they think their group is at on the continuum from serial writing to coauthorship. Of course, there is no single correct answer for this, but using the wiki's capabilities to show how authors are contributing to their pages can help. For instance, you could show how an initial sentence from one author was edited or completely revised in a later version of the page by one of the other authors. Better yet, show a place where a first author's ideas are built upon by a second author, who then contributes her own ideas to the piece. Point out groups that are succeeding in coauthorship by discussing scenarios that are developing into well-reasoned arguments, and have those groups discuss their writing process in front of the class. For instance, they may discuss how they are contributing their initial ideas and seeking feedback from group members, how they choose who will do surface-level editing and who will push for deeper revisions, and how they feel the overall text is developing.

Throughout the lessons, continue to discuss group norms, the expectations for how the final scenarios should read as full and complete texts, and how the group dynamics are supporting or impeding their work toward that goal. For instance, are some students participating too much? Too little? When disagreements arise, are group members all willing to negotiate civilly until reaching consensus? Is decision making shared among group members? By returning to these key concepts, you can help students self-regulate their writing process as individuals and as a group.

Also help make connections between what students are going through as authors and the topics at hand: copyright and intellectual property. Use questions like the following as the basis for writing assignments and deeper discussions:

- What about authorship? Who owns a collaborative piece? The initiator of the document? All the contributors, no matter what the contribution? The editors? The reviewers?
- Will there have to be a single, final author for each piece, or can the final product truly be considered an equal experience for grading? Should it be?

- In what ways can a group who feels that a member is not pulling his or her own weight approach that member and help him or her contribute more?

Engaging in inquiry and debate on such questions will make the topic of copyright even more real for students as they create their own intellectual property. Depending on the amount of time you have, a variety of follow-ups are possible, ranging from short writing assignments to collaborative multimodal projects, such as creating digital stories about particular instances of copyright infringement or public service announcements about legal places to download music.

Step 5: Wrap-Up and Assessment
(One Class Period, plus Grading Time)

Always a difficult process, assessment on a group project such as this becomes even more complicated. How and when do we assess the group? Individuals? The product itself?

As with most assessments, I decide what the formative tasks are that I want individuals to accomplish (for example, create your own wiki page, contribute significantly to the group's content, assist in peer review and revision) as well as the group to accomplish (for example, have a coherent scenario with a well-reasoned argument for your position).

In my home state of Michigan, there are standards for research, collaboration, and expository writing that can easily be monitored during the project and used to create criteria for a final, summative assessment of the group's scenario page. For instance, argumentative writing can be taught through minilessons that show students how to "resolve inconsistencies in logic; use a range of strategies to persuade, clarify, and defend a position with precise and relevant evidence; anticipate and address concerns and counterclaims; provide a clear and effective conclusion" (Michigan Department of Education's *High School English Language Arts Content Expectations*, www.michigan.gov/documents/ELA11-14open1_142201_7.pdf). These elements of argumentative writing can be built into the summative assessment as criteria in a rubric, thus reinforcing the idea and showing students that they are a critical component of their writing.

No matter what choices you make about formative and summative assessment, there are a few key ideas about copyright that students should reflect in their work:

- Do they make a compelling argument for or against fair use based on the four principles of purpose, nature, amount, and effect of use?
- Do they understand the difference between materials in the public domain, under copyright, and open to Creative Commons license?
- In what ways have they been able to appropriately incorporate public domain and Creative Commons materials into their work, especially if they have created multimedia?
- In what ways do they cite their sources? Are they using hyperlinks to documents that are on the Web and incorporating proper MLA (Modern Language Association) or APA (American Psychological Association) style?

These ideas could be used to develop an assessment rubric or could serve as the basis for reflection questions for students following the completion of the lessons. If you need help developing a rubric, you can use the free RubiStar rubric builder to get started (rubistar.4teachers.org/index.php). Finally, you may have students share their work in short, in-class presentations and/or comment on the work of others by using the discussion feature on their wiki page. These extensions would add some time to this step of assessment yet would also make the experience richer for students as viewers of and responders to the work of others.

Conclusion

While these lessons could come at any time, they would be ideal at the beginning of the school year as you establish norms for your classroom and collaboration, as well as what students should be doing to recognize and document their sources. Then, as they find images from Flickr to insert into their digital stories or as they choose music to play in the background of a podcast, they will have a firm understanding of what they can use and how. Returning to the scenarios throughout the school year with each new project you take on as a class will allow them to see that reading and writing in a digital age are complicated. They must evaluate the copyright provisions for each source and then efficiently document them. Moreover, this kind of research and writing positions them as collaborators more than paper and pencil ever did.

Once that ethos about copyright and intellectual property is established and guiding them, you can discuss other touchy topics such as plagiarism and cheating in a context where they understand the consequences, positive and negative, of integrating other people's ideas with their own. This contributes to the type of "problem solving, collaboration, and analysis" (2007, 1) that NCTE sees as critical to our students' academic, personal, and professional success. And creating these dynamic texts by collaborating with others, some people whom you don't even know, makes for a richer writing process and, in turn, better writers.

Appendix 2
The Digital Writing Workshop Study Guide

Chapter 1: Imagining a Digital Writing Workshop

- As you reflect on your experience teaching writing, what core principles do you value and enact in your classroom? Time for writing? Conferring with student writers? How have those practices remained constant over time?

- As you consider newer literacies and technologies that your students engage in outside of school, what effects do you feel they have on their academic literacies? For instance, do you feel that instant messaging is having a negative effect on student's grammar and spelling? In what ways do your opinions and your students' behaviors reflect what Knobel and Lankshear define as the two mind-sets, one more traditional and one that embraces new literacies?

- How do you hear the terms *digital* or *electronic* used in everyday conversation in your classroom and school? In the news? With your family and friends? What connotations do these terms carry, positive and negative? How do those connotations affect our response to using these technologies in our classroom?

- Given your own experience using technology for writing traditional and multimodal texts such as the PSAs students in Aram Kabodian's class were composing, what do you already know about "good" writing? What are the qualities of writing that make it good? How does this definition of good vary by purpose and audience for the work?

- Considering your own comfort level with teaching in a writing workshop and familiarity with a variety of technologies including word processors, digital audio and video editors, and online writing spaces such as blogs and wikis, what are some of the challenges you anticipate in trying to blend the principles of the writing workshop with these technologies?

Chapter 2: Fostering Choice and Inquiry Through RSS, Social Bookmarking, and Blogging

- Fostering student choice in genre and topic has been a hallmark of writing workshop instruction for years. What opportunities and challenges face you when you offer students choices? What curricular constraints are you under that may limit choices? In what ways can students have choices within limits and how can access to RSS readers, social bookmarking, and blogging inform those choices?
- When using an RSS reader, the information is inherently screened to some degree. What advantages and disadvantages does this offer your students as readers and researchers? In what ways might you encourage them to populate their RSS feeds with different kinds of information sources?
- Social bookmarking relies on the idea that people will share resources that are pertinent to others with whom they are networked. How does this filtering process affect the quality of the sites shared—for better or for worse? In what ways is using a social network better than simply looking for information through a search engine? In what ways could relying on social bookmarking be detrimental?
- Blogs offer opportunities for writers to share and categorize their work with tags as well as for readers to leave comments. In what ways will students have to frame their work so that they get the kinds of responses that they want? In what ways will students have to respond so as to give generative feedback and not simply offer the equivalent of a "good job" to their peers?

Chapter 3: Conferring Through Blogs, Wikis, and Collaborative Word Processors

- When you think about the process of conferring with student writers, what challenges do you face related to time, the kinds of responses you feel you can and should give, and helping students confer with one another?

- Blogs and wikis have been around for a number of years now, yet still carry certain connotations. What do you think of when you hear the term *blog*? *Wiki*? In what ways do these connotations affect our perceptions of these technologies as potential tools in the classroom?

- While the potential appeal for using technologies such as blogs, wikis, and collaborative word processors may entice students, what are some of the challenges that you may face—both in terms of access to the technology and teaching students how to respond appropriately to one another—that may be magnified by using these digital writing tools?

- Digital writing tools offer us unprecedented ability to confer with our students and offer very specific comments and feedback. How will you structure your own process of response so that you focus first on the writer, then on the writing, all the while using the features of the technology most effectively? For instance, how and when can you best use the comment feature on a blog post as compared to tracking changes in a collaborative word-processing document?

Chapter 4: Examining Author's Craft Through Multimedia Composition

- When we think of author's craft, what are the elements of writing that are most important to you? Leads? Elements of characterization? Dialogue? Conclusions? How do these elements translate into digital writing that is sometimes not print-based?

- How can the MAPS heuristic help you define the writing task for students as well as begin to think about assessment of the multimedia work that they will produce?

- For each of the three types of multimedia writing discussed in this chapter—photo essays, podcasts, and digital videos—what considerations would be most important in helping students craft a quality piece of digital writing? How do traditional categories we use to assess writing such as ideas, organization, or voice emerge in these pieces?
- In what ways can the distribution of these types of digital writing play into the academic purposes you have for assigning them as well as the motivations students have for creating them? What audiences and formats can you imagine for different kinds of assignments using these types of media?
- In looking at the examples of assignments from Reed and Murchie, what commonalities do you see in their pedagogical approach as well as their assessments?

Chapter 5: Designing and Publishing Digital Writing

- What publication rituals do you value in your own writing workshop? Public performances of writing? Anthologies of student work? Distribution to other media outlets such as fan fiction websites or newspaper editorial pages? In what ways can what you do already for publication be enhanced by the digital writing tools discussed in this chapter?
- Visit Helen Barrett's website on electronic portfolios and look at her categories of tools (electronicportfolios.org/categories.html). Besides blogs, what other tools might you consider using to have students create digital portfolios? Why would you choose one tool over another?
- As students create and share their writing via a wiki anthology, what other tasks could you imagine developing from that process? For instance, how might peer response groups develop? In what ways might outside audiences be able to contribute comments or offer revisions to student work?
- In creating audio anthologies for CD, also consider setting up a regular podcast for your classroom. In what ways might producing a weekly or monthly podcast featuring writers sharing their work (as compared to only creating a CD at the end) complement the types of publication and response that you are aiming for in your writing workshop?

Chapter 6: Enabling Assessment over Time with Digital Writing Tools

- What do you believe are the purposes of formative and summative assessment? In what ways do the digital tools outlined in the previous chapters offer you opportunities for these different kinds of assessment?
- In reviewing Figure 6.1, what additional lessons will you need to craft in order to meet the needs of your writers as they compose digital texts? Just as each bullet point in Burke's list can be turned into a minilesson and be considered a part of summative assessment, what other knowledge and skills related to digital writing will you need to gain in order to successfully teach about copyright, file management, file format, and distribution of digital texts?
- In reviewing Figure 6.2, what traits do you typically value in terms of student writing? To what degree does one trait outweigh others in your vision of assessment? How does that vision of assessment change with digital writing tasks?
- Examine Allison's "Be a Blogger" matrix (Figure 6.3). What is he asking his writers to do? In what ways do these tasks that blogging requires connect to the types of skills and dispositions outlined in the reports and curriculum documents about twenty-first-century skills mentioned in Chapter 4? In what ways does blogging help students become digitally literate?

Chapter 7: Creating Your Digital Writing Workshop

- Mishra and Koehler's idea of "Technological Pedagogical Content Knowledge" centers on the idea that effectively using technology in the classroom requires deep understanding of the content, the pedagogy, and the technology in order to make informed choices for student learning. What do you consider the "content" of a writing curriculum in the twenty-first century? How is it similar to and different from writing curricula in the past? How do specific technologies and pedagogical practices associated with those technologies affect the "content" of a writing classroom?

- How would you characterize your students' skills with technology as compared to their savvy related to Internet safety, privacy, and creative uses of those technologies? In what ways can we, as teachers who know and understand the writing process, contribute to their understanding of how to compose in digital spaces?
- Given the three elements of the framework in this chapter—your students, the subject of writing, and the spaces in which we write—how would you describe these elements as they are currently present in your classroom and school? What do you already have in place to begin your digital writing workshop? What else do you need to develop in order to make your digital writing workshop successful?

Appendix: Sample Lessons: Exploring Copyright Through Collaborative Wiki Writing

- Before exploring the resources on fair use and Creative Commons, write down or discuss your understanding of copyright law in general and, in particular, how it relates to educational use of materials. What are some of the "norms" that you understand about copyright (such as how long a clip of music can be or how long you can hold on to a videotaped episode of a TV show)?
- Visit the Media Education Lab's website (mediaeducationlab.com/) and view some of the resources available, in particular the page with resources related to the Code for Best Practices for Fair Use in Media Education (mediaeducationlab.com/sites/mediaeducationlab.com/files/CodeofBest PracticesinFairUse.pdf). How does this change your perception of fair use?
- What are your understandings of how a wiki works, both from a technical and a social standpoint? When someone mentions Wikipedia, for example, what is your initial reaction? How does that reaction influence your perceptions of wikis as a tool you can use for teaching writing?
- As students work to develop their projects, what are some of the questions that you think they will develop? What recent news stories about copyright might you be able to cite as examples for them to use?

References

Allison, Paul. 2009. "Be a Blogger: Social Networking in the Classroom." In *Teaching the New Writing: Technology, Change, and Assessment in the 21st Century Classroom,* ed. Anne Herrington, Kevin Hodgson, and Charles Moran, 75–91. New York: Teachers College Press and the National Writing Project.

Atwell, Nancie. 1998. *In the Middle: New Understandings About Writing, Reading, and Learning.* 2d ed. Portsmouth, NH: Boynton/Cook.

Aune, Sean. 2008. "Forget Word: 13 Online Word Processors." Accessed October 10, 2008, at mashable.com/2008/02/11/13-word-processors/.

Beach, Richard, Chris Anson, Lee-Ann Kastman Breuch, and Thom Swiss. 2008. *Teaching Writing Using Blogs, Wikis, and Other Digital Tools.* 1st ed. Norwood, MA: Christopher-Gordon Publishers.

Belanoff, Pat, and Marcia Dickson. 1991. *Portfolios: Process and Product.* Portsmouth, NH: Boynton/Cook.

Blog. Wikipedia, the free encyclopedia. Accessed February 17, 2008 at http://en.wikipedia.org/wiki/Blog.

Broad, Bob. 2003. *What We Really Value: Beyond Rubrics in Teaching and Assessing Writing.* Logan: Utah State University Press.

Burke, Jim. 2003. *Writing Reminders: Tools, Tips, and Techniques.* Portsmouth, NH: Heinemann.

Calkins, Lucy. 1994. *The Art of Teaching Writing.* 2d ed. Portsmouth, NH: Heinemann.

Center for Social Media. 2008. *Code of Best Practices in Fair Use for Media Literacy Education.* Accessed July 13, 2009 at www.centerforsocialmedia .org/files/pdf/Media_literacy.pdf

Cooper, Charles Raymond, and Lee Odell. 1999. *Evaluating Writing: The Role of Teachers' Knowledge About Text, Learning, and Culture.* Urbana, IL: National Council of Teachers of English.

DeVoss, Danielle, Ellen Cushman, and Jeffrey T. Gabrill. 2005. "Infrastructure and Composing: The When of New-Media Writing." *College Composition and Communication,* no. 1, 14–44.

DeVoss, Danielle, Troy Hicks, and the National Writing Project. Forthcoming. *Because Digital Writing Matters.* San Francisco: Jossey-Bass.

Dretzin, Rachel, and John Maggio. 2008. "Growing Up Online." *Frontline*. PBS.

Elbow, Peter. 1998. *Writing Without Teachers*. 2d ed. New York: Oxford University Press.

———. 2000. *Everyone Can Write: Essays Toward a Hopeful Theory of Writing and Teaching Writing*. New York: Oxford University Press.

Elbow, Peter, and Pat Belanoff. 2003. *Being a Writer: A Community of Writers Revisited*. Boston: McGraw-Hill.

Fletcher, Ralph J., and JoAnn Portalupi. 1998. *Craft Lessons: Teaching Writing K–8*. York, ME: Stenhouse.

Gere, Anne Ruggles, Leila Christenbury, and Kelly Sassi. 2005. *Writing on Demand: Best Practices and Strategies for Success*. Portsmouth, NH: Heinemann.

Gilster, Paul. 1997. "A Primer on Digital Literacy." Accessed March 2, 2008, at www.ibiblio.org/cisco/noc/primer.html.

Graham, Steve, and Dolores Perin. 2006. *Writing Next: Effective Strategies to Improve Writing of Adolescents in Middle and High Schools*. New York: Carnegie Corp. of New York.

Graves, Donald H. 1994. "Conditions for Effective Writing." In *A Fresh Look at Writing*, 103–14. Portsmouth, NH: Heinemann.

Graves, Donald H., and Bonnie S. Sunstein. 1992. *Portfolio Portraits*. Portsmouth, NH; Heinemann.

Haring-Smith, Tori. 1994. *Writing Together: Collaborative Learning in the Writing Classroom*. New York: HarperCollins College.

Herrington, Anne, and Charles Moran. 2009. "Challenges for Writing Teachers: Evolving Technologies and Standardized Assessment." In *Teaching the New Writing: Technology, Change, and Assessment in the 21st Century Classroom,* ed. Anne Herrington, Kevin Hodgson, and Charles Moran, 1–17. New York: Teachers College Press and the National Writing Project.

Hicks, Troy. 2008. "Exploring Copyright Through Collaborative Wiki Writing." *Classroom Notes Plus* 26 (2): 7–15.

Hicks, Troy, and Peter Kittle. 2006. Tapping the Social Nature of the Web in Collaborative Writing. Paper presented at the National Writing Project Annual Meeting, Nashville, November 17.

Hillocks, George. 2002. *The Testing Trap: How State Writing Assessments Control Learning*. New York: Teachers College Press.

Hunt, Bud. 2008, December 31. "Writing 1.0: An EduCon Conversation." Accessed May 26, 2009, at http://budtheteacher.com/blog/2008/12/31/writing_10_educon_conversation/.

International Society for Technology in Education (ISTE). 2007. The ISTE National Educational Technology Standards (NETS-S) and Performance Indicators for Students. Accessed May 20, 2009, at www.iste.org/Content/ NavigationMenu/NETS/ForStudents/2007Standards/NETS_for_Students _2007_Standards.pdf.

Kabodian, Aram. 2008. Digital Storytelling: Tales from the Real World. Paper presented at the National Council of Teachers of English Annual Convention, San Antonio, November 21.

Kajder, Sara B. 2004. "Enter Here: Personal Narrative and Digital Storytelling." *English Journal* 93 (3): 5.

———. 2007. "Unleashing Potential with Emerging Technologies." In *Adolescent Literacy: Turning Promise into Practice*, ed. G. Kylene Beers, Robert E. Probst, and Linda Rief, 213–29. Portsmouth, NH: Heinemann.

Kittle, Penny. 2008. *Write Beside Them: Risk, Voice, and Clarity in High School Writing*. Portsmouth, NH: Heinemann.

Knobel, Michele, and Colin Lankshear. 2006. "Profiles and Perspectives: Discussing New Literacies." *Language Arts* 84 (1): 78–86.

Kohn, Alfie. 2000. *The Case Against Standardized Testing: Raising the Scores, Ruining the Schools*. Portsmouth, NH: Heinemann.

Kress, Gunther R., and Theo Van Leeuwen. 2001. *Multimodal Discourse: The Modes and Media of Contemporary Communication*. London, New York: Arnold; Oxford University Press.

Lane, Barry. 1992. *After THE END: Teaching and Learning Creative Revision*. Portsmouth, NH: Heinemann.

———. 1999. *The Reviser's Toolbox*. Shoreham, VT: Discover Writing Press.

Lankshear, Colin, and Michele Knobel. 2006. *New Literacies: Everyday Practices and Classroom Learning*. 2d ed. Maidenhead, England; New York: Open University Press.

Lenhart, Amanda, Sousan Arafeh, Aaron Smith, and Alexandra Rankin Macgill. 2008. *Writing, Technology and Teens*. Washington, DC: Pew Internet and American Life Project and the College Board's National Commission on Writing. Accessed December 21, 2008, at www.pewinternet.org/ ~/media//Files/Reports/2008/PIP_Writing_Report_FINAL3.pdf.

Michigan Department of Education. 2006. High School Content Expectations: English Language Arts. Accessed May 20, 2009 at www.michigan.gov/ documents/ELA11-14open1_142201_7.pdf.

Mishra, Punya, and Matthew J. Koehler. 2006. "Technological Pedagogical Content Knowledge: A New Framework for Teacher Knowledge." *Teachers College Record* 108 (6): 1017–54.

Murray, Donald M. 1985. *A Writer Teaches Writing.* 2d ed. Boston: Houghton Mifflin.

National Commission on Writing in America's Schools and Colleges. 2003. *The Neglected "R": The Need for a Writing Revolution.* Accessed May 3, 2005, at www.writingcommission.org/prod_downloads/writingcom/neglectedr.pdf.

National Council of Teachers of English (NCTE). 2004. "Framing Statements on Assessment." Accessed January 5, 2009, at www.ncte.org/positions/statements/assessmentframingst.

———. 2004. "NCTE Beliefs About the Teaching of Writing." Accessed January 5, 2009 at www.ncte.org/positions/statements/writingbeliefs.

———. 2007. *21st-Century Literacies: A Policy Research Brief.* Urbana, IL: NCTE. Accessed December 9, 2007, at www.ncte.org/store/books/tech/128510.htm.

National Writing Project. 2006. *Local Site Research Initiative Report: Cohort II, 2004–2005.* Berkeley: National Writing Project, University of California. Accessed March 21, 2007, at www.writingproject.org/cs/nwpp/download/nwp_file/5683/LSRICohortIISummaryReport.pdf?x-r=pcfile_d.

———. 2008. *2008 E-Anthology: Summer Institute Writings and Conversations.* Berkeley: National Writing Project, University of California. Accessed March 2, 2009, at www.nwp.org/cs/public/download/nwp_file/6012/2008_E-Anthology_Overview.pdf?x-r=pcfile_d.

New London Group. 2000. "A Pedogogy of Multiliteracies: Designing Social Futures." Ed. Bill Cope and Mary Kalantzis, 9–37. New York: Routledge.

Newkirk, Thomas, and Richard Kent. 2007. "FAQ on Grading and Assessment." In *Teaching the Neglected "R": Rethinking Writing Instruction in Secondary Classrooms*, ed. Thomas Newkirk and Richard Kent, 64–86. Portsmouth, NH: Heinemann.

Northwest Regional Educational Laboratory. 2005. Assessment. Accessed March 2, 2009, at www.nwrel.org/assessment/.

The Partnership for 21st Century Skills designed in cooperation with the National Council of Teachers of English. 2008. 21st Century Skills Map: English. Accessed May 20, 2009 at www.21stcenturyskills.org/documents/21st_century_skills_english_map.pdf.

Pink, Daniel. 2007. "Japan, Ink: Inside the Manga Industrial Complex." *Wired* 15 (11). Accessed March 2, 2009, at www.wired.com/techbiz/media/magazine/15–11/ff_manga.

Pomerantz, Melissa Lynn. 2008. Beyond Time and Space: Using Audio Feedback to Help Improve Student Writing. Paper presented at the National

Council of Teachers of English Annual Convention, San Antonio, November 22.

Porter, Bernajean. 2005. *DigiTales: The Art of Telling Digital Stories*. Denver: BJPConsulting.

———. 2009. Personal Interview.

Putz, Melinda. 2006. *A Teacher's Guide to the Multigenre Research Project: Everything You Need to Get Started*. Portsmouth, NH: Heinemann.

Ray, Katie Wood, with Lester L. Laminack. 2001. *The Writing Workshop: Working Through the Hard Parts (and They're All Hard Parts)*. Urbana, IL: National Council of Teachers of English.

Reed, Dawn, and Troy Hicks. 2009. "From the Front of the Classroom to the Ears of the World: Podcasting as an Extension of Speech Class." In *Technology, Change, and Assessment: Teaching Practice in the Writing Classroom*, ed. Anne Herrington, Kevin Hodgson, and Charles Moran, 124–139. New York: Teachers College Press/National Writing Project.

Richardson, Will. 2006. *Blogs, Wikis, Podcasts, and Other Powerful Web Tools for Classrooms*. Thousand Oaks, CA: Corwin.

Romano, Tom. 2000. *Blending Genre, Altering Style: Writing Multigenre Papers*. Portsmouth, NH: Boynton/Cook.

Rozema, Robert. 2008. "Web 2.0: Blogs, Podcasts, and Feed Readers." In *Literature and the Web: Reading and Responding with New Technologies*, Robert Rozema and Allen Webb, 51–79. Portsmouth, NH: Heinemann.

Spandel, Vicki. 2005. *Creating Writers Through 6-Trait Writing Assessment and Instruction*. 4th ed. Boston: Pearson Allyn and Bacon.

Strickland, James. 1997. *From Disk to Hard Copy: Teaching Writing with Computers*. Portsmouth, NH: Boynton/Cook.

Strickland, Kathleen, and James Strickland. 1998. *Reflections on Assessment: Its Purposes, Methods, and Effects on Learning*. Portsmouth, NH: Boynton/Cook.

Swenson, Janet, with Diana Mitchell. 2006. "Enabling Communities and Collaborative Responses to Teaching Demonstrations." Accessed May 20, 2009, at www.nwp.org/cs/public/download/nwp_file/8965/Enabling_Communities_and_Collaborative_Responses_to_Teaching_Demonstrations.pdf?x-r=pcfile_d.

Tapscott, Don. 2008. *Grown Up Digital: How the Net Generation is Changing Your World*. 1st ed. New York: McGraw-Hill.

Tchudi, Stephen, and NCTE Committee on Alternatives to Grading Student Writing. 1997. *Alternatives to Grading Student Writing*. Urbana, IL: NCTE.

Wang, Caroline, and Mary Ann Burris. 1997. "Photovoice: Concept, Methodology, and Use for Participatory Needs Assessment." *Health Education and Behavior* 24 (3): 369–87.

Warlick, David. 2005. *Raw Materials for the Mind: A Teacher's Guide to Digital Literacy*. Raleigh, NC: Landmark Project.

Warschauer, Mark. 2006. *Laptops and Literacy: Learning in the Wireless Classroom*. New York: Teachers College Press.

Wiggins, Grant P., and Jay McTighe. 2005. *Understanding by Design*. Expanded 2d ed. Alexandria, VA: Association for Supervision and Curriculum Development.

Williams, Robin. 2008. *The Non-Designer's Design Book: Design and Typographic Principles for the Visual Novice*. 3d ed. Berkeley, CA: Peachpit.

Willis, Meredith Sue. 1993. *Deep Revision: A Guide for Teachers, Students, and Other Writers*. New York: Teachers and Writers Collaborative.

Wilson, Maja. 2006. "My Trouble with Rubrics." In *Rethinking Rubrics in Writing Assessment*, 1–9. Portsmouth, NH: Heinemann.

Writing in Digital Environments (WIDE) Research Center Collective. 2005. "Why Teach Digital Writing?" *Kairos* 10 (1). Accessed October 15, 2005, at english.ttu.edu/kairos/10.1/binder2.html?coverweb/wide/index.html.

Wysocki, Anne Frances. 2004. "Opening New Media to Writing: Openings and Justifications." In *Writing New Media: Theory and Applications for Expanding the Teaching of Composition*, ed. Anne Frances Wysocki, Johndan Johnson-Eilola, Cynthia L. Selfe, and Geoffrey Sirc, 1–41. Logan: Utah State University Press.

Yagelski, Robert P. 1997. "Portfolios as a Way to Encourage Reflective Practice Among Preservice English Teachers." In *Situating Portfolios: Four Perspectives*, ed. Kathleen Blake Yancey and Irwin Weiser, 225–43. Logan: Utah State University Press.

Yancey, Kathleen Blake. 2004. "Postmodernism, Palimpsest, and Portfolios: Theoretical Issues in the Representation of Student Work." *College Composition and Communication* 55 (4): 738–61.

———. 2008. Time to Leave the Ranch and Head for the 21st Century: Notes Toward a New Vocabulary and Set of Practices for a New Epoch in Literacy. Paper presented at the National Council of Teachers of English 98th Annual Convention, San Antonio, November 23.

Yancey, Kathleen Blake, and Irwin Weiser. 1997. *Situating Portfolios: Four Perspectives*. Logan, UT: Utah State University Press.

Index